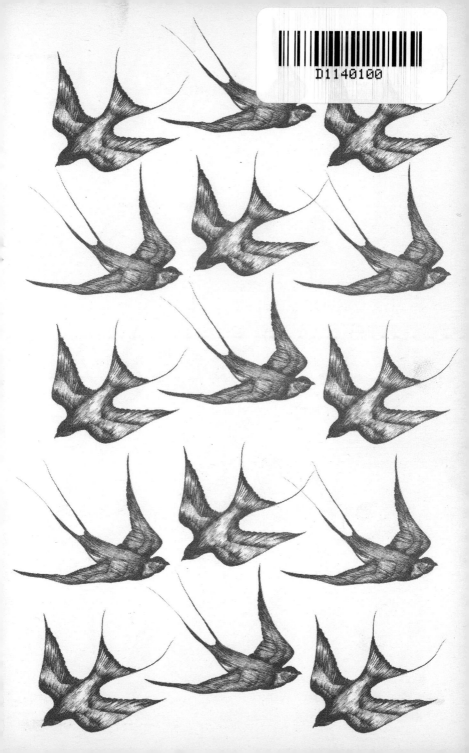

ALEX QUICK is the pseudonym of an English novelist. He is the author of *102 Free Things to Do*, *102 Ways to Write a Novel*, *102 Ways to Improve your Partner* and *102 English Things to Do*.

102
THINGS TO DO
IN SUMMER

Also by Alex Quick

102 Free Things to Do
102 Ways to Write a Novel
102 English Things to Do
102 Ways to Improve your Partner
102 Things to do in Autumn
102 Things to Do in Winter
102 Things to Do in Spring

First published in 2013 by Old Street Publishing Ltd,
Trebinshun House, Brecon LD3 7PX
www.oldstreetpublishing.co.uk

ISBN 978 1 908699 36 7

10 9 8 7 6 5 4 3 2 1

A CIP catalogue record for this title is available from the British Library.

Printed and bound in Great Britain

102
THINGS TO DO
IN SUMMER

ALEX QUICK

CONTENTS

1.

GO ON A ROAD TRIP

Summer is road trip season. It's the time to traverse the arteries of your country and feel its warm heartbeat. Go, just aimlessly, for the hell of it, or go for a reason (to attend a wedding or a festival), or go for seasonal work, or go to meet strange people. It's up to you.

First of all, check your car out. Get it serviced. Make sure you've got a full set of things like a spare tyre, jumper leads, oil, tools and a spare fanbelt. Brush up on your car maintenance, or find someone to come with you who is already brushed up.

Plan your trip, especially if it's important that you get back on time, want to see particular sights, or if you have to attend a particular event. Make sure you've got maps or GPS. Think about your overnight accommodation. You can book hotels on the road, day to day, or you can do it all in advance. Try not to over-plan, or the serendipitous element of your road-trip will be lost.

If you want to travel cheaply, sleep in your car or camp out. Bring a tent, sleeping bags, sleeping pads, bivouacs, cooking equipment. Also bring lots of food and water, since buying it along the way is going to be expensive. Bring everything, in fact, including the kitchen sink and draining board. The beauty of a road trip is that you don't need to go 'ultralight' (see §31).

Choose your companions carefully. Make sure they can all take turns driving. If you go on road trips with people you don't like, you will like them a lot less by the time you get back.

2.

CREATE A CROP CIRCLE

Crop circles are the fascinating designs wrought in standing grain crops by aliens, or perhaps by weather, or perhaps by humans with planks of wood and string. (The fact that numerous humans have admitted to their activities and even been filmed executing their designs makes the present author lean toward the latter hypothesis, but who knows?)

Perhaps the best way to decide is to have a go yourself. It should be noted that creating a crop circle is, strictly speaking, vandalism, unless permission is sought first from the farmer concerned. But given that permission has been secured, here's how to do it.

Find an open patch of standing grain, possibly near an ancient monument such as Stonehenge. Mark a central point with a stake in the ground and extend a string from the stake. Using a plank secured by ropes from the shoulders and extended like a plane's rudder-board, begin moving in a circle, flattening grain as you go. Move gradually inwards until the entire circle is flattened. Hey presto, a simple circle. For more complex designs, such as Mandelbrot sets or six-sided triskelions, take along a graduate maths student and some laser sighting equipment.

If you have worked hard on a design, you want it to be photographed from the air. Call a local helicopter tour operator, tell them about a mysterious formation that has appeared overnight and is far too complex to have been made by any human agency, give them the map reference, and hang up before they can ask too many questions.

3.

PLAY HANDBALL IN THE STREET

There are dozens of different types of handball. Some involve bouncing balls off walls, others involve hitting the ball into a goal or over a net. There is beach handball, Czech handball and Frisian handball. What they have in common is that they are all racquetless games, and involve striking the ball with the hand (sometimes fitted with a special glove).

Street handball is a rough-and-ready form of handball, usually played against a single wall. You can play against the side of a building or in a special handball court (essentially just an outdoor wall rigged out for the purpose). Players compete singly or in teams. Balls are usually of the baseball/tennis-ball size, but softer, so you can hit them with your unprotected hand without it hurting too much. The rules vary, but play commonly starts with one player serving against the wall. The ball is allowed to bounce once against the floor, but if the opposing player fails to return the serve by hitting it back against the wall, the server gains a point. Pretty simple! Courts are usually marked, so that a ball travelling beyond boundary lines, or going too short or long on the initial serve, is marked down as a foul. The killer shot is low down on the wall, so the ball bounces early and the returner can't get to it before the second bounce.

In summer you can play outside from dawn till dusk, until your hands are sore, your legs are aching and your voice hoarse. It's a simple, low-tech, beautiful game, and it proves that all you need to have fun is a little inventiveness.

4.

GO TO A WATER PARK

Also known as a sprayground. These are places where you play in water. There are pools, giant slides, tubes, tunnels, lazy rivers — water rides where you float along on rafts — fountains and splashpads. Some water parks also offer bungee jumping, human catapulting, artificial surfing and bodyboarding. They're most commonly for children, but they're also good for adults who still love having a wet and slippery time. They're reasonably cheap, and you can stay there all day if you want to. Take your own lunch. Perfect for summer!

A recent development in water park design has been to provide more sophisticated waterscapes for adults, where you can walk through mist, amble in fountains, relax in saunas and steam rooms, or lounge in interconnected hot tubs. Or you can play on the hydraulophone. This is a musical instrument in which water pressure is generated in a tube: the player creates sound by blocking and unblocking a series of holes. It's rather like playing a very sweaty flute. Hydraulophones are sometimes free-standing (they can also be played in a concert environment) or they can be fitted to the sides of pools and hot tubs.

If nothing else, going to the water park will force you – and your children if you have any – to disconnect from Facebook and email for a while, as electronics and water don't mix.

5.

COOK SOMETHING IN A SOLAR OVEN

A solar oven is a device that requires no electricity, no gas and no nuclear power. It's totally green. It's just a box with a reflector that concentrates the power of the sun. Solar ovens are simple to make and they really work, though you need a hot sunny day for good results.

First you will need two cardboard boxes: one smaller, one bigger. You'll also need a sheet of clear plastic or glass, some newspaper, some tinfoil and some black paint.

Nest the two boxes so that they fit inside each other with about a two-inch gap all around, and insulate the gap with balled-up newspaper. Now line the internal box with tinfoil and paint its bottom black (this absorbs heat). Put the glass over the top of the whole assembly so that any heat that goes into the box is trapped inside (as in a greenhouse).

Now you need to make some reflectors. Glue more tinfoil on another piece of cardboard and fit it to the top of the box, angled towards the sun. The sun will strike the reflector and bounce into the box, where it will be trapped. You can use reflectors on all four sides if you wish to maximize heat.

Anything can be cooked in a solar oven, but dishes such as stews and casseroles do well because they require long, slow cooking.

A solar oven demonstrates the infinite generosity our local star. A meal cooked in a solar oven is the ultimate free lunch.

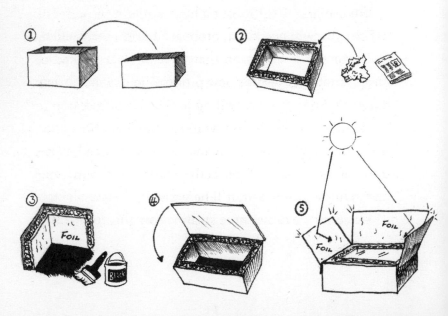

6.

GO DUMPSTER DIVING AND HAVE A PICNIC IN THE PARK

This sounds like odd advice, since you can easily make a picnic from the nice things in your fridge, or buy something from a shop: but the beauty of dumpster diving (or freeganism) is that you never know what you are going to be eating.

Supermarkets throw out a huge amount of perfectly edible, undamaged food, often well within its sell-by date, for no other reason that they are overstocked or need to make space for new product lines. It's all there for the taking if you're willing to do a bit of research in back alleys. You will find wrapped Belgian chocolates, unblemished apples or bananas, loaves of bread, cakes and biscuits, etc.: all perfectly wholesome, nutritious fare. Unless you nab it, it'll be wasted.

Once you've done some stealthy foraging and you've

got the haul in your rucksack, take it to the park and spread it out on your picnic cloth. Add a bottle of something or other (drinks are rarely found in dumpsters), lie on the grass and enjoy the sun. Share your food with people passing by. Tell them you found it round the back of a supermarket and see their reactions. People will say things like: 'How do you know there's nothing wrong with it?' Reply: 'Just look at it! That's the easiest way to tell!' If they're still not convinced, offer them a mandarin orange. Mandarin oranges come with their own built-in protection system, called peel. Next, they'll take a cake, and it'll all be over.

7.

SHOWER UNDER A WATERFALL

Showering under a waterfall is cold and painful compared to showering at home. But then again, life isn't about doing things that are easy!

First of all, you need to find a waterfall. I'd recommend you start off modestly. Don't begin with Victoria Falls, because the hippopotami are bothersome, and the water pressure will render you unconscious. Something a few metres high is ideal: big enough to be spectacular, but small enough to be serviceable. Secondly, consider wearing shoes. The environments around natural waterfalls are often slippery, and the water will knock you off balance and onto rocks if you're not careful. Thirdly, don't use so much soap and shampoo that you create floating islands of foam. Frogs have to drink that stuff!

Buddhist monks meditate under waterfalls: the discipline is known as *takishugyo*, or 'waterfall training'.

The waterfall is symbolic of the insistent demands of the phenomenal world. Apparently it's harder to have evil thoughts when a column of water is thundering onto your head.

After your shower, explore the lakes, pools and rapids around your waterfall. These can be beautiful to swim in, especially the more turbulent Jacuzzi-like ones.

When you get home you might wish to take a domestic shower to remove leeches and soothe cuts and bruises, but it will have been an invigorating experience.

8.

TAKE PART IN COMPETITIVE LIFESAVING

Every year an alarming number of people are drowned in the sea, in rivers and lakes, and in swimming pools. And even in the bath. Water safety and lifesaving techniques, involving training in rescue, resuscitation and first aid can help reduce these deaths.

Lifesaving is also a sport practised worldwide. Lifesavers compete in a variety of events, including flood and river rescue, ice rescue and swimming pool rescue, in which teams and individuals try to match each other for speed and skill.

Lifesaving may be the only sport that has a serious moral purpose, though one should perhaps include lawn bowling.

There are lifesaving clubs and organizations country-wide: it's rather like being back in the Scouts or

Guides, only as an adult. The sport is overseen by the International Lifesaving Federation (ILS). Perhaps amusingly, many completely landlocked countries such as Switzerland, Macedonia, the Czech Republic and Austria are members of the ILS.

9.

MAKE YOUR OWN SOLAR PHONE CHARGER

Solar phone chargers can be bought off the shelf, but they're not always cheap. The good news is that you can make one yourself.

Let's say you have a basic phone that needs 5 volts to charge up (this will apply to most phones and portable MP3 music players). First of all, find a phone charger that fits your phone – the kind that plugs into the wall. Cut the plug off it and strip down the two wires to expose them. Solder each wire to a small square of adhesive copper tape (each square being about 1cm on each side). Now stick the tapes with the wires attached to the two inner jaws of a clothespeg. Take eleven solettes (very small cut-up pieces of solar panels about a few centimetres long each), stack them up and spread them out so they look like a miniature lady's fan. (Not a fan for a miniature lady but a miniature fan for a normal-sized lady.) Clamp the clothespeg with the copper tapes to the base of the fan. The positive terminal goes at the bottom and the negative terminal at the top. (There are only two ways to do it!) Now plug the jack into your phone. Take the mini-array out into the blinding summer sunlight. Power your phone on. What does the display say? Phone charging? Yes! You're charging your phone on nothing but the sun.

All the components can be bought cheaply online or at discount electrical outlets. It won't come out at night, but given this limitation, the sun will supply all the electricity you can use.

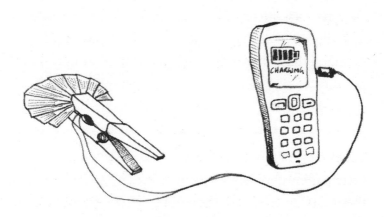

10.

START YOUR OWN CHARITY

In summer, people are at a loose end, the weather is great, and there's optimism in the air: it's the ideal time for charity fund-raising.

Maybe you've already identified what needs to change. Are public areas dirty or uncared-for? Are people lonely or homeless? Is there petty crime? Illness? Lack of education or art? Draw up plans for how you would remedy the problem and how much money you will need. Talk to people and find out whether they share your opinions. Then think about actually raising the money. Consider events such as sponsored treks, parachute jumps, cycle rides, skip-a-thons or moustache-growing. Approach family, friends, work colleagues, neighbours; get help from spiritual organizations, schools, youth groups, interested parties. Create awareness on social media. Write to award-giving bodies. Contact celebrities who might lend their name to your cause or donate funds. If you're running a charity for bronchitis sufferers, contact famous bronchitics. Register your group with the authorities so that you can call yourself a charity and reap the benefits.

One tip: don't do it *entirely* alone. Find trustees who feel as passionately as you do. The energy they bring to the project will help you when you're flagging, and they'll have ideas you could never have come up with on your own.

11.

WALK AMONG THE DEAD

Most people, if asked about the top ten most beautiful spots in their town or city, would ignore their local cemetery. They'd be dead wrong.

Cemeteries – especially large, Gothic ones with lots of hidden spots – are wonderful places for a summer stroll. In towns they're often the greenest and wildest open spaces, havens for wildlife: if you want to see birds, foxes or even deer, sit in a big urban cemetery for a while. All animal and all human life is there. Joggers rub shoulders with mourners and lovers, and they all seem to get along. Cemeteries and graveyards somehow manage to strike the right balance between decay and growth, past and future, gloom and optimism. What are graves after all, but testaments to the reality of human love? Cemeteries are incomparable places for meditation, not necessarily on death, but on life. They bring things into perspective. Research published in the *Personality and Social Psychology Bulletin* in 2008 found that just being physically near to a cemetery affected how willing people were to help a stranger. And the stones, mausolea and monuments are endlessly fascinating, from overweening obelisks for Victorian businessmen to tiny wooden crosses for paupers. Of the many lessons graveyards teach us, one is that there's no democracy in death.

Except, of course, that it's the ultimate democracy.

12.

SELL YOUR BOOKS ONLINE

You want a new summer read but you're hesitating on shelling out. Meanwhile your shelves are groaning with books you know you'll never read again: *Let's Go Vietnam 1979*; *The Physics of Alice in Wonderland*, *Modern Javanese Short Stories*. Or you've just done your summer-term exams and you want to get rid of your old coursebooks. There are people out there who want these books, and they're willing to pay high prices.

There are various forums for sellers. The biggest names are Amazon and eBay, but you might have luck with Etsy, Powell's, WeBuyBooks, Alibris, Biblio or any of dozens of others. In most cases it's quick and simple to register as a seller.

Three tips for those starting out:

1. Check regularly to see what other sellers are doing, and price accordingly. You can use re-pricing software that automatically adjusts your prices up or

down according to movements in the market.

2. Be honest. If you list a book as being in Very Good condition when it's actually only Fair, you will attract bad reviews which will damage your sales in future. Condition is everything. A Very Good copy with a dust-jacket may be worth a dozen times as much as a Fair copy without one.

3. Ship promptly first-class, and advertise this as a selling point.

After you've exhausted your own unwanted tomes, look for bargains at garage sales, book auctions and library sales. You may find bookselling is addictive.

13.

DISCOVER A SUMMER READ

There are two times in the year when book-buying and book-reading go into hyperdrive: summer and Christmas. Publishers and booksellers fall over each other to produce the biggest summer or seasonal blockbuster, and the 'gift book' comes into its own.

In summer we are constantly being told what to read by the people whose job it is to sell us books. But if we only bought what they wanted us to, our literary diets would consist entirely of celebrity memoirs, TV tie-ins and cookbooks. Somewhat indigestible.

We might do better looking elsewhere for recommendations. How about libraries? Many libraries provide lists of books for summer reading. Books to read on the beach, books for learning new skills, books for children bored at home. These lists can give you ideas, but for something more personalized, ask a librarian. Librarians love being asked for advice. Can you recommend a historical novel set in Pompeii? If they can't give you exactly what you're looking for, they'll probably be able to suggest something close.

Or what about joining a book group this summer? You'll end up reading things that you would never have read otherwise. You might plough your way through them with gritted teeth, or end up wondering how you could ever have survived without them. You'll expand your critical skills, meet new people, drink their wine and see inside their houses.

14.

ATTEND A HIGHLAND GAMES

The most venerable Highland Games are held in August at Dunoon, Argyll, Scotland, but there are other games held throughout the world, particularly in the USA, where the crowds regularly dwarf those in Scotland. Games are also held in Brazil, Canada, Hungary, Switzerland and elsewhere (though not in England, which would be invaded if it tried it).

The most spectacular event is undoubtedly the caber toss: in this, the object is not to fling the caber (a tree trunk) as far as possible, but to 'turn the caber', meaning to make it rotate end over end and land in such a way that it points away from the tosser in a 12 o clock position. But there are many other events: the *Maide Leisg* involves two kilted types sitting opposite one another, the soles of their feet pressed together, each grasping a stick held horizontally between them: on a given signal each attempts to pull his opponent off his feet. Then there is the sheaf toss: this involves using a pitchfork to throw a hay bale over a high bar – useful if you need to feed very tall animals.

The Games are a celebration of Scottish and Gaelic culture in general. As well as games, they feature Gaelic music, Highland dancing, displays of weaponry and traditional arts, and Scottish cuisine. Haggis will be high on the menu, though in the USA you might find yourself eating a tartan-themed corn dog.

15.

MAKE WINE

You can make wine out of anything – old socks, if you want. The important thing is the sugar content of your starter brew. Sugar, through the action of yeast, turns into alcohol. But fruit makes it taste nicer.

The fruit of choice for centuries has been the grape, mainly because grapes have a high juice content and can produce a range of complex flavours. Many home wine-makers don't use grapes, though, preferring to experiment with new flavours.

So, take the fruits you've decided to try – strawberries, watermelon, kiwi fruit, whatever you have handy – pulp them, and strain the pulp through a sieve. Get the brew as free of pulp as you can, because excess pulp will lead to problems with sediment later on. Transfer to a fermenting bucket, and add wine yeast (available from home brew shops) and sugar. Use a hydrometer to check that the amount of sugar will bring the finished brew up to the right alcohol strength. The strongest wines will be about 14 percent proof. Summer is a great time to make wine, because a warm ambient temperature will aid fermentation; even so, you might also need to buy a fermenting belt to warm up the bucket.

When fermentation is almost complete (after three or four days), siphon the wine into a demijohn, and continue fermenting gently for a week or two. The wine should clear. Now transfer to bottles.

It's very tempting to drink your wine too early, but it really will improve if you 'lay it down' for a month or two. If you drink it straight out of the bucket, it will lay you down.

16.

LEARN TO SURF – AND NOT THE INTERNET

Surfing is like flying without wings. It's the sort of thing non-surfers experience only in dreams.

First you'll need a surfboard, and a wetsuit if the water's cold. Now choose a beach. A good beach for absolute beginners will have waves that break about 2-4ft (around 1m) high. Wade into the water, then lie on your belly on the board. Using a crawl stroke, paddle out to the zone where the waves are swelling but not yet breaking. Now turn the nose of your board towards the beach. When you see a good wave coming, paddle hard, so you are positioned just before the wave and matching its speed as it approaches the break-zone. On your first few tries you should stay flat and ride the wave lying down, but soon you're going to want to try standing up. Practise this on the beach first. The stand-up manoevre is known as the 'pop-up', and it's achieved by gripping the sides of the board and doing a push-up, then tucking your legs underneath and getting to your feet. Adopt a crouch stance, as low as possible, with hands out for balance. Too far forward on the board and you'll nose dive. Too far back and the wave will pass ahead of you.

When you start, it seems impossible that you could ever balance on a bit of plastic with a mass of turbulent water seething and churning under you.

Even if you never master it, you'll get a beautiful tan.

17.

MAKE FRESH FRUIT RAINBOW POPSICLES

Shop-popsicles are generally not very interesting, either in taste or appearance. But if you make your own, the sky's the limit: literally, if you make them in rainbow colours.

You'll remember from school: ROYGBIV. Red, orange, yellow, green, blue, indigo, violet. So, for example, strawberries for red, oranges for orange, pineapple for yellow, grapes for green, blueberries for blue, and dark grapes (cheating slightly) for indigo and violet. Find some popsicle moulds – the big ones are best – and put the fruit, whole, in the mould in order of colour, filling the moulds all the way to the top. Now take some lemonade – home-made is best, with just lemon juice, sugar and water – and pour into the mould, filling up the gaps between the fruit. Pop the lid on, freeze for a couple of hours, and they're ready.

Alternatively, for a smoother popsicle that is still rainbow-coloured, you can liquidize the fruit first, in individual batches of red, orange, yellow, etc., and freeze each batch. Before the liquid is completely frozen, transfer it in slushy globs into your popsicle mould to make your rainbow.

Rainbow popsicles are not the only possibility, of course. Popsicles are frozen art-objects in their own right, fruit trapped in amber: pineapple juice with floating mango chunks, tangerine and loganberry with grape-juice, banana and cumquat surprise. All utterly delicious on a hot day.

18.

SKIP STONES

Stone-skipping is a popular outdoor pastime around the world, and in summer there are festivals of stone-skipping for otherwise respectable adults.

There are two ways to measure success in skipping a stone: you can go for distance or you can go for number of skips. The former is the approach taken at the Annual World Stone-Skipping Championships held at Easdale, Scotland, and the latter by the North American Stone-Skipping Association (NASSA) of Franklin, Pennsylvania.

Whichever you choose, distance or skip-count, a number of variables are considered important. First, the water. A smooth, calm surface is vital, so a lake or a calm river is a good bet. Secondly, the stone itself. This should be about the size of the palm of your hand, flat and smooth, and not perfectly round: if it is angled it will be easier to grip and thus easier to impart spin.

No spin, no skim. Thirdly, posture. You should stand sideways onto the water and get your throwing arm down low. Fourthly, the throw: you should aim to hit the water at around a 20 degree angle for maximum bounce. Any more or less than this and the stone will either sink immediately, or bounce high into the air and sink on re-entry.

The world record holder for number of skips is Russell 'Rock bottom' Byars, who achieved 51 skips on 19 July 2007 at Riverfront Park, Franklin, beating Kurt 'Mountain man' Steiner, who had held the previous record of 40 skips.

Stone-skipping is also popular in Sweden, where they call it '*kasta macka*', or 'tossing a sandwich'.

19.

SPOT BIRDS

The feathered creatures that surround us can become the focus of a lifetime's study, even a lifetime's obsession (which will involve the purchase of some very big lenses and a camouflaged thermos). I'm not suggesting you go that far. Just take some time to get to know the brilliant, delicate little flecks of life that inhabit the world around us.

Birds have personalities. Who, for example, isn't drawn by fascinated disgust to the cuckoo (also known regionally as the cog, geck, gowk or tittling), which infiltrates the nests of birds such as the meadow pipit or reed warbler and parasitizes them, dooming their offspring to death by ejection from the nest. If two cuckoos are laid in the same nest, the stronger of the two – still blind – will also eject its weaker sibling, showing a ruthlessness that would make Richard Dawkins blench. Or consider the common mallard, which has an extraordinary sex life. Ducks can and do change their gender: male ducks, given the right conditions, grow the feathers and adopt the behaviour of female ducks, and female ducks can morph into male ducks. Ducks are the bird world's drag artists.

Some birdspotters will glance at a ball of brown feathers half a mile away and say confidently 'chiffchaff'; but this is mere showing off and nothing to do with birdspotting. Real birdspotting is not a competitive sport but a way of attaining peace with your surroundings, understanding and appreciating them.

If you think that there aren't any birds near where you live, just go out and sit in the garden for a while. Be very still, and they will come to you.

20.

SLEEP OUTSIDE

Tents are not really necessary in summer. If the weather is warm, if the forecast is dry, if you have warm clothes and a sleeping bag, why bother with a tent?

It's really a question of why you're camping in the first place. If it's to get close to nature, don't sequestrate yourself under polyester. Out in the open, you can see the stars, feel the warm breeze, listen to the sounds of the night, and most wonderfully of all, experience the dawn.

First of all, you'll need a sleeping bag and some sort of groundsheet (such as a sleeping pad). You could also use a bivy sack, a sort of outer sock to your sleeping bag, which provides additional insulation and still leaves your head uncovered.

Choose a sheltered place, perhaps under a tree. Don't sleep outside in places that are too exposed to the wind, such as hilltops. Mind you, if it did get too cool, you could always just move downhill.

If you sleep outside you'll be vulnerable to mosquitoes and other biting insects, so take some insect repellent and work it in all around your neck and behind your ears.

If you're a long way from home and you have food with you, put the food at some distance from your sleeping-place so as not to attract wild animals to your bed.

Or sleep on the beach, with a campfire next to you. There is nothing more orthopaedic than warm sand.

21.

CATCH CRABS ON A LINE

This is about the simplest way to harvest live creatures from the sea. Nothing is needed except a piece of string, some bait and a net. No hook, no rod, no reel, no copy of *Angling Today*.

First of all get some raw meat. Chicken leg or neck meat is fine, but you can also use beef, turkey, squid... crabs aren't too choosy. Cut off a fairly big hunk – about the size of a golf ball, say – and tie it securely to a line. You can use string, but anything will do – fishing line, baling twine, anything that's strong. Then find a casting-off point. Crabs reside in the sea, of course, but also in lagoons and estuaries. Position yourself on a jetty, seawall or bayou bank, or just wade into the water. Throw out the line a few yards from where you are standing. Then wait.

When you feel a tug on your line, you've caught a crab (hopefully it's a crab: if it's a shark, drop the line).

The crab is holding the meat with its claws and is nibbling at it. Now begin to pull in your line. Do this very, very gently, an inch at a time, so the crab doesn't get suspicious. As soon as it gets close enough, net it. Put it in a coolbox or basket (crabs can survive for a long time out of water but live longer if they're iced). Then simply re-use the line and bait.

Wear gloves while you're handling your catch. A tip: they nip.

22.

GO TO A CHAINSAW CARVING FESTIVAL

Making sculptures with chainsaws is a hugely skilled – and dangerous – craft, requiring many months of training and a Certificate of Chainsaw Competence. It's not something that can really be attempted on a whim. But if you're chainsaw-curious, why not attend a chainsaw-carving festival? These often come up in the summer months (chainsaw carving is usually performed outside) and the noise of roaring saws, the flying sawdust and the smell of wood is irresistible.

Chainsaw carving is practised throughout the world, though it is particularly popular in the USA, Australia, Germany and the UK. It's not uncommon for crowds to top 10,000 at some of the larger events. The level of precision and detail possible with a tool designed to lay waste to forests is astonishing, and most festivals feature a wide range of subjects and styles. (Only one subject remains unpopular – a tree.) Sculptors compete with one another to win prizes, and the sculptures are sold off at auction. At many festivals there are usually also demonstrations and lessons.

Sculptors are free to carve any design they like, though one chainsaw festival gives the following guideline: 'Unless the competition has a stated theme, competitors are allowed to carve as their fancy pleases. However, competitors should bear in mind that members of the public and children are attending the event, and thus they should consider matters of taste and decency. Any sculptures considered offensive will be removed and may be burned. We do however allow nudes that are executed with propriety.'

23.

LIE IN BED WITH SOMEONE LISTENING TO A SUMMER STORM

Turn the lights out. Take someone to bed – a friend, relative, lover or pet – stroke their hair softly, and look into the cool gunmetal of their eyes. Don't say anything. The thunder will speak for you. Don't move. Lightning will make your shadows dance on the walls. The room will fill with the smell of wet dust. Ions will tickle your tongue and make the hairs on your body bristle. Wisely, you have left the windows open and the curtains are getting wet: a pool is forming on the floor. A cool breeze is blowing over you both, the cool of all the world's water. Don't say anything. The rain is speaking for you. In the distance, glowing blood vessels fissure the air. God is going through the roof.

When you are ready, find your loved one's hand

(or paw). Whisper: 'Let's go outside'. Then, without stopping to gather raincoats, shoes, hats, Wellington boots or other barriers between you and the tempest, tiptoe out of the house, as if afraid of waking someone. Enter the storm. You are drenched in seconds.

24.

MAKE ROSE PETAL PERFUME

What is perfume for? Well, it's for spending a lot of money on. The recipient knows you have spent a lot of money and is grateful.

If you make your own perfume, however, the recipient knows you haven't spent a lot of money. You have to rely on the fact that your perfume smells really really nice. This is how to make sure it does.

First, cut four large sweet-smelling roses. Strip the petals off and place them in a saucepan. Then fill the saucepan with two cups of water. Bring to the boil. Simmer for half an hour with the lid on the saucepan.

After half an hour, remove from the heat and allow to cool. Strain out the rose leaves, and then filter the remaining liquid through some finely woven fabric. Due to evaporation you should now have about a cup of perfume left (and your house will smell very lovely). Put this back in the saucepan and boil it further until only about a quarter of a cup remains. Cool the mixture again. To this, add a tablespoon of surgical spirit (also called rubbing alcohol, and available at chemists). This will enable the rose perfume to volatilize when it is placed on skin. Place the concoction in an old perfume bottle or sprayer.

You can try this recipe with other flowers, such as jasmine, lavender, lilac or honeysuckle, or you can mix these other flowers with the roses.

25.

GO SHEEP RACING ON SARK

Sark is a small outcrop of the British Channel Islands: it is 3 miles (5 km) long and 1.5 miles (2.4 km) wide at its broadest point, and is accompanied by two smaller companion islands, Little Sark and Brecqhou. It has a population of around 600 people. No cars are allowed on the island, and the only transport is by bicycle, tractor or horse. On Sark, July is sheep racing season.

Sheep racing is conducted over a course of around

100 yards (100 m) featuring various jumps and hazards. The sheep are kitted out with jockeys in the form of teddy bears or knitted mascots, and are individually numbered. A flock going at full pelt is quite a spectacle: sheep can reach 40 mph (64 kmph), so woe betide anyone who stands in their way. And they jump pretty well too: sheep are surprisingly gracile, given the chance, managing bounds of around 4 yards (4m). They are not known as the brightest of animals, of course, but given enough training and incentives, they can usually find their way to the finishing tape. Bets placed in the 'sheepstakes' go to charity.

If you can't make it to Sark, there is sheep racing at other locations around the world. Moffat in Dumfriessshire, Scotland, hosts an annual sheep race, and Methven in New Zealand is the home of the 'Baa Blacks'.

26.

VISIT A MAIZE MAZE

The maize maze is an example of a pun generating a multi-million pound industry. The basic idea is that in summer, maize (corn) farmers create mazes in their crops and invite paying guests to negotiate their way through them. It's rather like crop circles, except that the patterns are not always circular and the farmers are not the victims but the perpetrators. If you doubt that it really is a multi-million pound industry, find out how many maize mazes are in your area. By August they begin springing up everywhere. Such is the popularity of maize mazes that there is even a Maize Maze Association, the official body representing maize maze constructors, which holds a conference every year on maize maze issues and where guest speakers give presentations on the state of the industry and network with each other to drive traffic towards their nutritious puzzles.

The beauty of maize is that it really is possible to get lost in it. Crops such as wheat or barley only reach to the waist at best, whereas maize can reach above adult head height. It's like Hampton Court with cobs. And if you get tired of maize there are usually plenty of other things to do: you can pet animals, play Krazy Kroquet, climb a hay tower, go Kart racing, and partake of refreshments. You can visit jungle-themed mazes, alien-themed mazes or dinosaur-themed mazes.

In short, there is more to maize than cornflakes.

27.

DIP A POND

Pond-dipping is the business of fossicking around in ponds and pools and finding out what minibeasts lurk there. It's fun for kids, but adults, under the pretext of supervising them, can have a lot of fun too.

You'll need a net with a long handle, a couple of white plastic trays, a spoon, a magnifying glass and a field guide to pond fauna.

Firstly, take the net and move it around near the bottom of the water for a minute or so. Don't go too deep or you'll pick up a lot of ooze. If you scoop near the edges of the pond you will stand more chance of picking up creatures feeding on water-plants. Then take your haul and transfer it to one of the white plastic trays. (Pre-fill the trays with water so the beasts have something to breathe.) The trays should be white, or at least light-coloured, so it is easy to distinguish the interesting specimens from the gunge. When you spot something suggestive, use the spoon to transfer it to the second tray.

Now take your guide and identify what you've found. You might have snails, Pond Olives, leeches, Pond Skaters, Great Diving Beetles, White-Clawed Crayfish, tadpoles or dragonfly nymphs. All are readily identifiable.

Don't forget to put them back afterwards. They are not very happy kept in a jar, and may turn on each other out of boredom; you will be left with one very fat Great Diving Beetle.

28.

WALK BETWEEN TWO CITIES

If you're fond of the road less travelled, this is for you.

Hikers and backpackers tend to head for the same places: beauty spots, hills, trails, coastal paths, and so on. The result is that these places are all jammed up with people wearing fluorescent backpacks. If you walk between cities, you won't experience any of these people, because they're all taking trains to get to the place where they want to start walking.

Here's how to do it. Let's say you want to walk between Norwich and London, a distance of 120 miles (193 km). Buy six maps that between them cover the entire route, patch them together and draw a pencil line from one city to the other. Now cut out a two-mile-wide corridor with the pencil line in the centre. Following footpaths, you'll be able to zigzag from one side of the line to the other.

Take the minimum of equipment (see §31, 'go

ultralight backpacking'). One recommended method is to take nothing but a credit card, some plasters, a change of underwear and a phone. You can arrange to stay at bed-and-breakfast accommodation as you go.

When you arrive at your destination you will have got to know parts of your country that few people (apart from the ones that live there) ever see.

29.

LEARN ALL SIX OF THE BASIC SWIMMING STROKES

The first of the six basic strokes is the crawl. This is performed by lifting the arms in turn up and over the head and then finger-tip first into the water. Snatch a breath on the side of the raised arm.

The butterfly: lay on your front, raise both arms out of the water simultaneously, then plunge them into the water to drive yourself forward. At the same time propel yourself with a dolphin kick (in which the legs are together and undulate like a dolphin's tail).

In the breast stroke, lie on your front and point both arms forward just under the surface of the water. Then turn your hands outwards and pull your arms to the side, making a frog kick.

The side stroke involves laying on your side in the water, reaching forward with the lower hand, and sculling with the upper hand. It's used particularly in rescue situations.

In the backstroke, lie on your back and bring your arms over your head, slicing them little-finger first into the water while kicking with your legs.

The doggie paddle: just put out your paws, palms downwards, and push the water down to keep yourself afloat, kicking freestyle with your legs.

Why does one always feel pleasantly tired and relaxed after swimming? It's because swimming is the most complete form of exercise, working all the muscles of the body in a weightless environment where no one muscle is put under too much strain. It's the perfect way to develop fitness.

30.

CATCH, KILL, GUT, COOK AND EAT A FISH

Right there by the riverbank. It's a beautiful sunny day, and it's trout season. A tug on your line: you reel it in. And what a beauty it is, wet, iridescent, spraying droplets of water as it thrashes on the pebbles.

A tap on the head, and it's out cold. Take the hook from its mouth. Lay it on the bank. Now take your knife and make an incision from the vent all the way up the belly to the gills. Grab the guts at the gill-end and pull them out. Now clean the inside with running water (from the river – pretty convenient). Trout don't need de-scaling, so that's one less job to do. Now start a small fire. Get it going until you've got some embers. Wrap the fish up in a double layer of tinfoil (remove its head first if you prefer) and just place it in the fire: it'll cook right through in ten minutes. Alternatively skewer the fish on a stick, poke one end of the stick in the ground so the fish is suspended over the fire, and roast it like a marshmallow.

Or you can take it home and pan-fry it with mushrooms, garlic and white wine.

This all presupposes that you know how to fish, of course, but it needn't be a major problem. Many trout hatcheries cater to people with no equipment or skills and will hire out rods for the day. In some places you can even catch trout in small pools with a net, and the proprietors do the rest for you.

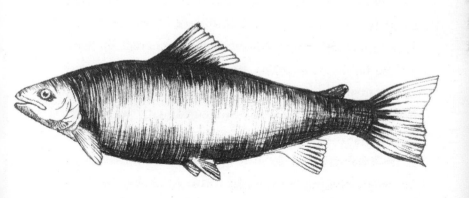

31.

GO ULTRALIGHT BACKPACKING

Hiking and backpacking are fun summer activities, but a heavy pack can turn your trip into a purgatory of sore muscles, chafed shoulders and aching feet. If, on the other hand, you take measures to lighten your load, you will be better placed to enjoy the scenery, cover greater distances, and reduce injuries.

Ultralight backpacking was pioneered by Emma 'Grandma' Gatewood in the 1950s. On her now-legendary hike of the 2,168-mile Appalachian Trail in 1955 (aged 67), she managed with just a duffel bag, a plastic shower curtain and a blanket. Ultralight backpackers who have followed in her footsteps have made reducing pack-weight into an obsession.

The heaviest common items are sixfold: tent, sleeping bag, clothing, water, food and the backpack itself. These can all be trimmed down. A tent (with its double insulation layer, groundsheet, metal poles etc) can be replaced by a simple bivouac-style covering sheet to keep off the rain. Special lightweight sleeping bags can be purchased with all the insulation on the top layer, which traps heat where it is needed. A bubble-cell roll can be carried for ground insulation (similar to Grandnma Gatewood's plastic sheet). Spare clothing can be minimized. Water (which is very heavy) can be collected in streams along the way and purified. High-calorie energy bars minimize weight and don't require cooking (which also obviates the need for cooking apparatus). And a very light backpack with no frames completes the picture.

The complete picture, with everything you need for survival and protection from the elements, may weigh as little as ten pounds (4.5kg). Just make sure you do it in summer!

32.

GO METAL DETECTING ON THE BEACH

Most people use the beach for recreation, but the beach is also a source of treasure.

Go on summer mornings before pleasure-seekers have arrived, and you will have the place to yourself. Small, well-attended beaches are particularly good, because finds are more numerous and the search area is smaller. Start by identifying the 'towel zone': that strip of beach above the high tide mark where bathers put their towels down. Coins, jewellery and other metal objects will be buried at fairly shallow depths. Groynes and sea-walls (people use them for shelter), the underneaths of piers (ne'er do wells prowl there), or sand-dune paths (tired holidaymakers struggle along them, dropping things) are also good places to look.

For historic finds you need to go closer to the sea and deeper. Most beaches are formed of more than one stratum: sand at the top, with clay, sandstone or bedrock underneath. Objects work their way down to the harder layers and rest there. If you look for evidence of erosion elsewhere on the beach you will see what sort of sub-surface stratum to expect. Or wait for storms. Storms will often erode large sections of beach overnight, churning up the sand and bringing long-buried objects into detecting range.

If you find things that are valuable and obviously recent (rings, bracelets, watches), be a darling and turn them in to the police. There may be a reward.

33.

STAY UP ALL NIGHT FOR THE DAWN CHORUS

In summer, it's hardly bedtime before the sun is due to rise again. Why not stay up all night and wait for the sun to rise before going to bed? Take a walk to the top of a hill, maybe with a friend, sit in the warm grass, wait and have a midnight picnic, and share some stories. Don't get too drunk, or you'll fall asleep.

In midsummer, the sky begins to lighten at around half past three. Then, some time before dawn, the birds start to sing. Birds are obsessed with sex and real estate, but it doesn't make it any the less beautiful. This is the only chance they get to be free of the noise-pollution of man, and they grab the opportunity with gusto.

See how many species you can identify. Birds will often start singing in order. First there is the syrupy

gurgle of the blackbird, then the fluting warble of the robin, then the braying of the wren.

At around half past four the first golden beams strike up from the hills, and the chorus reaches a climax. The sun breaks free of the horizon and floats improbably into space. There's no one awake to see it except you.

Another day has begun. You still have another three hours before anyone is even awake. Pack up your things and trudge sleepily down the hill.

34.

GO SKINNY-DIPPING

First of all, plan a party near a body of water. If you don't have a lake or ocean nearby, a swimming pool or a hot tub will do.

It's as well to plan this with a group of like-minded friends, since casual acquaintances generally don't appreciate being pressured into stripping off. Make sure it's dark, either by having the party at night, or if indoors, by turning the lights down low. Same-sex groups probably work best. Make sure everyone is relaxed and happy first, then invite people in for a swim. If people are reluctant, tell them you might have a spare costume hanging around, or that they can use yours. The offer might be enough to get them to throw their inhibitions to the wind. Tell them 'If you've got it, flaunt it.'

If you're throwing the party, the buck stops with you, i.e. you get buck naked first. Tell everyone you're going to lead the way, then just calmly, confidently take your clothes off and plunge in. From the safety of the water, invite your friends to join you.

The main thing is to have fun. Don't cajole anyone who doesn't want to. It's very liberating being in your birthday suit in the water, but if no one finally wants to join in, don't make waves.

35.

MAKE AN ICED GREEN TEA LATTE

Iced tea is wonderful on a hot day. And it's easy to make. Just boil some water, steep some teabags, and refrigerate. You can add sugar and citrus flavourings if you like.

But for a slightly different summer tea drink, why not try an iced green tea latte made with traditional Japanese matcha tea?

Matcha tea comes in a light green powder and can be bought in sachets at oriental food shops. It's the tea used in the famous Japanese tea ceremony and has a distinctive rich, thick texture when combined with water or milk: in fact, in Japan, matcha is used to flavour a myriad of products, from cakes and candies to sushi and snacks.

So, to make a matcha tea latte, mix three quarters of

a cup of milk with one teaspoon of matcha tea powder and one tablespoon of water. Put them in a bowl and mix them throroughly with a whisk: you may wish to sieve the powder first to make sure there are no lumps. If you don't have a whisk, try blending the mixture in a cocktail shaker or even a plastic bottle with the lid on.

When the tea is blended (a minute or so of whisking or shaking should do it), strain the mixture over some ice-cubes in a tall frosted glass.

Very relaxing after a long sizzling day!

36.

GO COCKLING

Cockles are delicious in a variety of dishes: the French serve them with cod, the Italians with spaghetti and garlic, and the Welsh with laver bread. They make tasty soups, stews and even salads. And harvesting them is easy.

Cockles live buried in sand or mud in tidal or estuarial areas, and should be collected at low tide. This can be done at any time of the year, but it's nicer in summer. A good indication of a place rich in cockles is simply where you can see cockles scattered over the surface: these will be cockles that have not yet dug themselves in, or have been disturbed by birds. Broken cockle shells are also a good clue. Buried cockles will also leave shallow depressions in the sand, giving it a pock-marked look.

Taking an ordinary garden rake, work backwards, raking up the sand to a depth of an inch. This will uncover the cockles, which can be picked out and put in a bucket. You can also strain your raked sand though a garden sieve to ensure you don't miss any.

You should always be aware of the tides in the area where you're cockling, and if you are planning to go far out, check for forecasts of fog or other bad weather. Always carry a mobile phone or radio device, wear high-visibility clothing, and give yourself enough time to get back to land. You may also need to get a permit, so check with your local authority.

37.

MAKE A TIMELAPSE FILM OF A SUNFLOWER

You can plant sunflowers at any time from spring to late summer. If you start them off from seed you can track their progress from the moment they poke their way out of the earth to the point where they are grazing the firmament. But if you want to make a timelapse film, it's probably best to shoot the whole thing indoors. You might like to try dwarf sunflowers, which don't grow much over a couple of feet high, and can be grown in pots indoors or in a greenhouse.

First of all, you need a camera with a built-in 'interval shooting' function (many digital cameras have this as standard nowadays). Turn all the settings onto manual, particularly the white balance, because if the camera adjusts each shot for lighting conditions you will end up with a flickering effect. Now punch in your settings for shutter intervals and for the total time of your movie. Go and make a cup of tea (or several) and let the camera do its work. When the sequence has finished, take the photos and export them to a video editing program. This will enable you to stitch all the images together into a timelapse film.

Despite popular belief, sunflowers don't 'track the sun' during the day, but orientate themselves in a roughly easterly direction during their adult lives. You'll notice some spectacular effects as the flowerheads bloom.

38.

MAKE A COLA OR ROOT BEER FLOAT

This is a classic summer recipe, and it's very easy to make. All you need is ice cream, some soda drink, and a glass.

There are several ways to do it, but they all rely on the fact that ice cream is lighter than water and will float to the top of the glass. Try it this way: take two or three scoops of vanilla ice cream and put them in a chilled glass. Add around half a glassful of your soda drink. Cola and root beer work well, but you might want to use cream soda, grape soda or any other flavour. The ice cream will react violently to the soda, producing masses of bubbles that will threaten to spill over the lip, so pour slowly. As the bubbles rise up, the ice cream will feel gravity's bonds loosen and will lumber to the top of the glass. Add more soda to top it up, and perhaps some chopped nuts, maple syrup or chocolate sauce. A straw, and you're ready.

For a more 'milkshake'-like effect, you can blend the ice-cream and soda mixture together first, pour it into your frosted glass and then top off with more ice-cream, more soda and other toppings.

As well as varying the flavours of the soda you can vary the flavours of the ice-cream. A cola and vanilla ice-cream float is called a 'black cow'; a cola and chocolate ice-cream float is called a 'brown cow', and a grape soda and vanilla ice-cream float is called... well, it doesn't have a name yet. 'Purple cow' anyone?

39.

MAKE A BENDER

What do you do if you go camping and you forget your tent? Or it blows away?

Benders are simple dwellings made of tree-branches. They've been used for centuries as a form of shelter for woodfolk, hunters and forest labourers. They're tents for people who wouldn't know what a 'tent' was.

First, clear the area where you want to make your bender. A square with 12ft (4m) sides should do nicely. Then find 12 thin branches, about 7ft (2.2m) long each, and with a diameter of about 2 inches (5cm) at the base. Coppiced hazel, ash or willow is fine. Using a sharpened stake, make a foot-deep (30cm) hole in the ground and insert one of your branches (thickest end) into the hole. Repeat the process four times, spacing the holes at around 2 foot (60cm) intervals. Now make a parallel row about 6 foot (1.8m) away. You should now have eight branches reaching into the sky.

Take opposite pairs of branches and bend them down towards each other to form an arch. Tie each pair of branches at the apex with string. Now you have a tunnel! Take your remaining four branches and thread them through the arches for extra stability. Now take a canvas or tarpaulin. Lay it over your bender and fasten it at the edges with stones.

You are ready to take up residence. Put in a carpet, some lamps and a portable TV. Make a bed (raise it from the ground for extra warmth). Hang some pictures on the walls. Well-built benders are highly resilient structures and will last for years.

40.

PUT YOUR ELDERFLOWERS TO GOOD USE

...that is, by making elderflower cordial. The elder blossoms from around the end of May to July, so elderflower cordial breathes the very essence of summer.

First find your flowers. The elder bush is impossible to mistake for anything else: its flowers grow in large spreading clusters formed from hundreds of white florets, spreading out in a flat lacy cone. Snip off around thirty of these flowerheads. (Try to find an elder bush that is remote from traffic, since otherwise you might end up with a petrol-flavoured brew.)

Now make your syrup base. Mix 2¼ pounds (1 kg) of granulated sugar with three pints (1.5 litres) of water, bring to the boil and cool. Chop some citrus fruit. Two lemons and two oranges should do, but you can also use limes or any combination of fruits.

Wash the elderflower heads and add them to the cooled syrup. Also add 2oz (55g) of ascorbic acid, available at chemists or home-brew shops, which will stop the mixture losing its pale pond-water colour. Steep the mixture for 48 hours and strain through muslin or a pair of tights. Transfer to bottles and refrigerate. If the bottles are sealed, the cordial will keep for months.

Elderflower cordial is delicious cold on its own, of course, but it can also be mixed with sparkling water or wine.

41.

MAKE SOURDOUGH BREAD

Sourdough bread is most famously associated with San Francisco: the yeast that is used to make classic San Francisco sourdough is actually called *Lactobacillus sanfranciscensis*. It's the ideal bread to make in summer, because the dough requires a long time in warm temperatures to rise.

Sourdough tastes sour not because (as some people imagine) the baker adds yoghurt or lemon juice to the dough, but because the bread ferments in a very special way: the dough is leavened by lactic acid bacteria as well as yeast, both of which are vital to the process.

To make sourdough you first need a starter culture. You can make this yourself with just flour and water (whole grain flour is best); you can also use orange · juice or unsweetened pineapple juice instead of water to give more acidity. Keep the starter at approximately 24 degrees throughout the process, and natural bacteria and yeast within the flour will start the process of fermentation. Begin with 2 tbsp of flour and 2 tbsp of juice, and add the same amount of flour and juice to the mixture every day for four days. By the end of the fourth day you will see it bubbling.

To make the dough itself, mix 1 cup of whole wheat flour, 2½ cups of ordinary bread flour, 1 tsp of salt, 1½ cups of water and ¼ cup of the starter mixture. Knead, and allow to rise for around 18 hours at 24 degrees, during which time the dough will double in size. Bake in an oven with a tray of water on a lower shelf to give added moisture, and spray the dough with water before baking.

Serve with traditional San Fancisco fare such as clam chowder and sand dabs!

42.

GO TO WOMAD

WOMAD began at the instigation of Peter Gabriel (formerly of the band Genesis), Thomas Brooman and Bob Hooton. WOMAD stands for World of Music, Arts and Dance, and it's the biggest international music festival on the planet. Its first incarnation was in 1982 in rural Somerset, featuring acts such as The Drummers of Burundi and Echo and the Bunnymen (who played together live on stage), but since then it has expanded enormously, and has held over 160 events worldwide, in countries including Abu Dhabi, Australia, Austria, Canada, Denmark, England, Estonia, Finland, France, Germany, Greece, Ireland, Italy, Japan, New Zealand, Portugal, Sardinia, Sicily, Singapore, South Africa, Spain, Turkey, the UK and the USA. Wherever you live there's likely to be a WOMAD festival somewhere near you. Many of them take place in summer, notably the biggest UK festival, now held at Charlton Park in Wiltshire.

WOMAD has had some spectacular successes in identifying world-class artists before they were ever known to a global public – names such as Nusrat Fateh Ali Khan, Neneh Cherry, the Asian Dub Foundation and Youssou N'Dour spring to mind. And it never stays still: one of the most extraordinary recent events was the 1996 Great Musical Rail Journey of Australia that crossed the Nullarbor desert, stopping off for a performance in the outback of Pimba.

The incredible appeal of WOMAD is its determination to challenge boundaries and bring people together in a celebration of our common humanity. If there is a single most effective way of challenging racism, WOMAD has got to be it: a demonstration of the unifying power and joy of music, arts and dance.

43.

MAKE A SAND SCULPTURE

The simplest sand sculpture is a pyramid. It bears its weight well, isn't prone to collapse, looks good, and can be built quite high with the aid of a few helpers. But when you've completed your first pyramid you might be ready for a new challenge.

The key to making complex sand sculptures – forms such as human figures, buildings, faces, VW Beetles, or indeed anything else that you can imagine – is *compaction*. You need first of all to create a mass of highly compacted sand that can then be carved, much as a sculptor carves a figure from a block of marble. So, if you wish to create a sand Madonna, first create a block of compacted sand that could contain a sand Madonna. There are various ways of doing this. The easiest is to use the 'paddling pool' technique. First of all, clear a circular area and build a little sand wall around it like a paddling pool. Fill it with water and stamp down the sand inside. Then add more sand and water and repeat, building up the wall as you go. When you've finished, remove the outer layers of wall, and you will have an internal core of hard sand.

Now you can start to carve. Begin your carving from the top so as to prevent waste sand from falling onto the lower portions of your design. If you've done your compaction work well you can even undercut the design without too much danger of collapse.

One note of caution as you work on your master-piece: don't build too close to the sea! Nothing is more dispiriting than to see your beautiful VW Beetle having its tyres washed away.

44.

WANG A WELLY

The world Welly Wanging championships are held every June in the village of Upperthong, West Yorkshire. The sport involves throwing (or 'wanging') a Wellington boot as far as you can. The rules are too extensive and complex to give in full here, but some highlights include:

Distances shall be measured in yards, feet and inches.

The standard welly shall be the Dunlop green, size 9, non steel toe-cap. Competitors shall select whether they use left or right welly.

No tampering with the welly shall be allowed. Factory finish only. No silicone polish is to be applied.

A maximum run-up of 42 paces shall be allowed. This distance was chosen in memory of Douglas Adams, himself a proponent of the sport.

The welly shall land within the area defined by the

straight lines between the Upperthong Gala field and Holme Moss television mast on one side, and on the other by the line between the field and Longley Farm windmill. This playing area is known as the 'Thong'.

The use of wind assistance is allowed and, indeed, encouraged. Waiting for a suitable gust, however, is limited to one minute. No artificial or man-made wind is to be used.

Welly wanging is also practiced world-wide: the town of Taihape, New Zealand, has proclaimed itself 'the gumboot capital of the world'. Unsurprisingly, Upperthong and Taihape are twinned.

45.

OPEN YOUR GARDEN TO THE PUBLIC

Why should you allow strangers to tramp around your backyard? Well, for charity. Various organizations around the world run open garden programmes. In the UK, it's the National Gardens Scheme, and in Australia it's Open Gardens Australia. It doesn't matter whether your patch of land is a courtyard, a cottage garden or a 300-acre parkland estate with gazebos and ornamental mazes: as long as it can provide visitors with a few points of interest (enough, say, to merit a half-hour visit), you qualify. If you have some rare or unusual plants, or a good shed with some intriguing evidence of a bizarre hobby, or some chickens, then so much the better. If you can offer tea and cake, so very much the better. Visitors to gardens seem to regard tea and cake as an essential part of the experience and will probably make bitter remarks about your dahlias if you don't provide them.

If you don't have a garden, then you can become a volunteer. Open garden programmes, because they are non-profit-making, are always looking for volunteer labour to sell tickets and refreshments.

If your garden is too small and dull, or if you are nervous about opening to the public, you can team up with a neighbour. But it's best to bear in mind that people don't expect perfection. They are there to support a good cause, and an immaculately trimmed lawn and slug-free sunflowers are not mandatory.

46.

SELL YOUR POEMS

You might prefer to try this in summer. It's pretty wretched to stand around trying to sell your poems in winter, and on a sunny day people might be more receptive.

You need *chutzpah* to do this – but no more than for, say, busking. And you might conceivably make more money. Someone who certainly did make a living out of it was the American poet Vachel Lindsay. In March 1905, Lindsay, who was at the time an impoverished art student, asked his teacher if he would ever cut it as an artist. The teacher tactfully replied that he would do better trying to sell his poetry, and so Lindsay, either in desperation or inspiration, rushed off some copies of his poems and took them out in the streets of Manhattan. Pricing them at two cents each, he earned 15 cents on the first day (one doctor paid 5 cents for two poems), and was elated. He bound his oeuvre into the collection *Rhymes to be Traded for Bread* and began a series of tramps all over America bartering recitals for food and shelter. His first trek was in the spring of 1906, ranging on foot from Florida to Kentucky, traversing some 600 miles, selling poetry readings as he went. He became famous, read for Woodrow Wilson and his cabinet, was praised by WB Yeats, and published several further collections.

If you want to try it, print off some copies of your favourite pieces, price them competitively, and simply approach people with a winning smile. 'I wonder if you'd like to buy a poem,' you might say. 'I can give a reading first, no charge.'

47.

WATCH BABY SEA TURTLES HATCH

There are marine turtles in every ocean of the world except the polar seas; so beaches where turtles spawn are found on all continents (except Antarctica). This doesn't mean it will be easy to see turtles hatching where you live, but with a little effort it shouldn't be impossible. In the USA, South Carolina and Florida are notable for sea turtle spawnings; in Europe they can be seen in Greece, Cyprus and Turkey. Most spawnings take place in summer.

Female sea turtles often lay eggs on the beaches where they themselves hatched, so nesting and hatching sites can be constant over many millennia. The females typically lay their eggs at night, digging a hole around half a metre deep and depositing a clutch of up to 200 eggs. These gestate for around two months, and the sex of the baby turtle is determined by the warmth of the sand in which it is laid (warmer sand, more females). At a given moment, the hatchlings all chip their way out of their eggs using a special tooth evolved for the purpose, and head for the sea. This almost always takes place at night, when there is less risk of predation, but even given this precaution, very high numbers are eaten by birds and other animals before they can make it the safety of deep water.

Why watch turtles? For one thing, it can actually help them. Most species of marine turtles are endangered, and turtle tourism can spread awareness of the fact. Tourism encourages local communities to protect the turtle in their own interests, rather than hunting it for food, leather and jewellery. Turtle conservation is one of the greatest successes of ecotourism, in fact. Book your turtle holiday now!

48.

GO ZORBING

What could be more absorbing than to go zorbing? Summer is not complete without a good zorb. You can zorb singly, or romantically in pairs; in the largest zorbs, two couples can comfortably zorb. In short, when you're tired of zorbing, you're tired of life. Zorbing makes the world go round. Literally.

Zorbing, invented in the 1990s in New Zealand, involves rolling down hills in inflatable transparent plastic balls. Each zorb is constructed with an inner and outer skin separated by compressed air, so that the zorber is protected during the ride by a spherical shock-absorbing blanket (zorbing is also known as sphereing). The zorber enters and exits through a small tunnel in the side of the zorb, which has led some to draw comparisons between a zorb and a womb; the zorb-cavity is often filled with water, which acts, like amniotic fluid, to reduce friction. Sometimes zorbers are strapped into their womb and at other times are allowed to tumble and flounder freely as the zorb careers on its way to the bottom of of the hill. There have been no zorb-related fatalities: perhaps alone among extreme sports, zorbing is thrilling, bizarre, hilarious, unique – and safe. And zorbing is fairly ubiquitous: there are zorbing courses in the UK, USA, France, Germany, Australia and lots of other countries.

Oddly enough, the world record for fastest zorb is held by the cricketer Freddie Flintoff, who completed a 100m zorb-run in 26.59 seconds in 2012.

49.

GO TUBING

Tubing started, it is said, on the private lake of the Princess Panthip Chumbhot of Nagar Svarga in Thailand. Tubing involves riding the water on giant inflated inner tubes. The sport was massively pumped up by the Princess's patronage and is now enjoyed around the world.

The tube-rider sits with their buttocks in the hole of the tube and their legs and back resting on the sides. These days, tubes are custom-made for the sport, and it is unusual to find any old car inner tube being used. Modified tubes have handles at the side to allow the tuber to hold on for the ride and are often fitted with a rubber skin covering to protect the tuber's bottom grazing on hazards.

There are many types of tubing, but tubing on water can be divided into two categories: towed tubing and free tubing. In towed tubing, the inner tube is towed by a watercraft such as a motorboat: speeds approach those experienced by waterskiers, so tubes have been known to take to the air, sometimes deliberately, sometimes not, and not always with happy consequences for the tube-rider. Free tubing, where the tuber floats down a river, is more sedate, at least potentially, though shooting rapids in a tube looks pretty scary.

A variant of tubing often encountered in summer sports is tubing on plastic slopes, such as artificial ski-slopes. This is skiing without the control, grace or dignity, with your bottom in a giant doughnut, but it's a lot of fun.

50.

BECOME A MINIATURE GOLF PRO

Mark Twain said that golf was 'a nice walk spoiled'; miniature golf could be characterized as 'a spoiled walk spoiled even further with the addition of huge clown faces, windmills and tunnels'.

Mini-golf, or crazy golf, or goofy golf, or Tom Thumb golf, or midget golf, is a staple of seaside and holiday entertainment around the world, and there are an estimated 15,000 courses globally. You can play it inside or outside, in barns, hotels and casinos, or on the roofs of buildings (the most famous course in London is on the roof of Selfridges's department store, and features London landmarks in the form of giant cakes). In the heyday of mini-golf, from the 1930s to the 1960s, the gimmicks were truly outlandish: one American course involved putting your ball though a cage of bears who were trained to try and stop it.

What is the point of crazy golf? Well, it takes all the forbidding aspects of golf – the heavy and expensive equipment, the club membership fees, the interminable waits for other players, the extensive rule-book, the aspirational class-consciousness – and eliminates them, making it cheap, fun, democratic, child-friendly and resolutely pointless (rather than merely being actually pointless). Screaming and cheating are not only allowed but expected. Anyone can play, and anyone does.

51.

RENT A ROWBOAT

Boating is among the cheapest and most enjoyable of all summer activities, and there will almost certainly be a lake or river near you that hires out rowboats by the hour.

Being on water on a sunny day is both immensely pleasurable and immensely aimless. You're not going anywhere, and you always come back to where you start from. But this is part of the charm. 'Just messing about in boats', as Jerome K Jerome put it, is reason enough for engaging in the activity,

It's a curiously isolating experience to float with a companion in the middle of a large body of water. The rest of the world and its noise drops away, and there are just the two of you, poised on a thin skin of wood or metal over unknown depths. This tiny thrill of peril and isolation makes it the ideal time for an intimate conversation – perhaps a marriage proposal. It might also be a good time to attempt a murder. (And the ideal blunt instrument is at hand – two of them, in fact.)

Even if you don't have any personal declarations in mind, a boat is a great place to do other things – you can have a picnic lunch, for example, or compose a novel. A rowboat in a lake is also a good vantage point to spot birdlife, since many waterfowl are not observable from the shore, and will come up to your boat if you provide them with crusts.

52.

GO PUNTING

A punt is a long, flat-bottomed boat that you propel with a pole. You can do this from the back or from the front: at Oxford they traditionally do it from the front, while at Cambridge they do it from the back. On a sunny day, with the willow warblers chirping gently in the oaks, there is no finer activity than to take to a punt and glide silently along a river, exploring its little tributaries with their overhanging branches and lily-dappled pools, or find a landing place and lie on your back (possibly with a loved one), watching the clouds drift absent-mindedly in the azure sky.

Of course, this summer, you may be neither at Oxford nor at Cambridge, which is a shame, but don't let it stop you going punting. Many other places have punts. You can go punting in London (on the Regent's Canal); in Durham; in Bath; in Sunbury; or in other places around the world, such as Christchurch, New

Zealand; Denver, Colorado; or the Okavango Delta, Botswana (where your punt will be called a *makoro* and you will have to watch out for marauding hippopotami).

The *London Magazine* of 1828 had a good many things to say about punting, and among the best was this: 'It will give a particular relish to success, if you be successful, and wonderfully dull the edge of disappointment, if the contrary be your fate, if you never take punt (for we recommend that as the easiest mode of exercise) without stowing therein a sufficient basket of ham, tongue, veal pie, stilton-cheese, bottled ale and porter, port, sherry, moselle, claret, brandy, and cigars.'

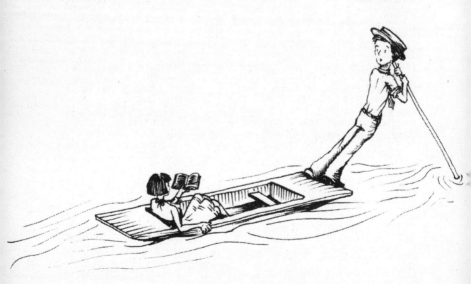

53.

WHISTLE THROUGH A BLADE OF GRASS

If you happen to be in the Okavago Delta in a *makoro*, one simple way to scare off hippopotami is to whistle through a blade of grass.

Well, that may not exactly be true. But blades of grass have been used by hunters in the past to imitate the cry of distressed animals. When predators come to look for the distressed animal, they can be shot.

Your motives may be more benign, though – just to produce a funny noise on a summer's day. Here's how to do it. The first thing you need is a good blade of grass. Find one that's flat: one that is round or ellipsoid in cross-section will not work. Then place it between the balls of your two thumbs at the top. Letting the grass hang down between bent thumbs, grip it with the base of your thumbs and pull it taut by straightening your thumbs. Now you have a good taut blade. Purse your lips, put them hard up against your hands, and blow into your thumbs and across the blade. This should produce a very loud, keening shriek.

The key thing is to get the blade taut. It's like a guitar string: only a tightened string will sound a note.

For advanced practitioners it's possible to get a range of notes by varying the tautness of the blade with your thumbs, so you can play 'The Green Green Grass of Home'.

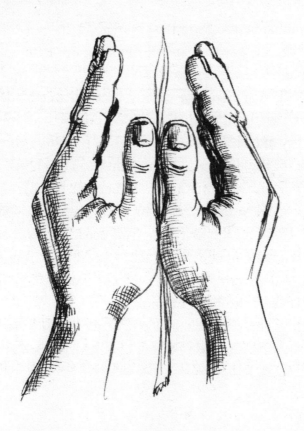

54.

CREATE A BUTTERFLY GARDEN

Butterflies, beautiful, harmless, evanescent butterflies, are the embodiment of summer. And they're easy to attract.

To start your butterfly garden you need to bear two important things in mind. Firstly, butterfly larvae (caterpillars) need somewhere feed. Secondly, butterflies themselves need somewhere to find nectar. So you need two types of plants, host plants and nectar plants, and the two are not usually the same. For example, the Swallowtail likes to lay its eggs on milk parsley, which give its larvae a good food source; but for nectar, it prefers bluebells, thistles and teasels. The Peacock butterfly (the one with the spectacular eye-pattern wings) lays eggs on nettles and hop plants, but prefers dandelions, hawkweed and marjoram as a nectar source (so, in the case of the Peacock, you can combine a butterfly garden with a herb garden). Check for the most common butterflies in your area, and look up their preferred plants for the larval and adult stage. A good rule of thumb is to choose nectar flowers that are very open, so that the butterflies can get to the nectar easily: Buddleias, Marigolds and Hydrangeas are very good, as are Black-eyed Susans and Lavender. Plant them in bunches to make a tempting display.

A few other tips: plan your butterfly garden in a sunny area that is sheltered from wind. Include some sort of water source in your garden (butterflies get thirsty). Butterflies also like large flat rocks where they can warm up. Don't use slug bait, even the eco-friendly type, as it will kill the caterpillars (and other insects) too.

Or you can interpret the task entirely differently and build a garden in the shape of a butterfly. Just don't forget to put some good butterfly plants in it.

55.

PLAY CHESS IN PUBLIC

Chess is a long, brooding game played amid a sepulchral silence. Wrong! It's a loud, fast, raucous game with hands smashing down on timers, opponents sledging one another between moves, and banknotes changing hands. Many major cities have chess districts – places for public chess such as parks, cafes and pubs. You can play surrounded by rollerbladers, buskers and kids on bikes, or in a noisy bar where you have to scream the word 'checkmate'. You can play blitz chess with a five-minute limit – or a three-minute or one-minute limit. Or you can play on a giant chessboard. The biggest playable chessboard in the world is at the Malampuzha Garden, Kerala, India, though you need to be pretty strong to move the pieces.

Chess is incredibly democratic. All ages, races and genders meet on equal terms. You never know who's going to sit opposite you. You might even bump into a grandmaster.

If you don't know the moves, you can pick them up in half an hour. And however many games you play, it will always be different. The trillionth game of chess, perhaps played on a space station around Neptune, will be different from the first, and so will the quadrillionth.

56.

LEARN TO PLAY THE GUITAR

Guitars and summer go together. You can play a guitar in the park, on a street corner, or around a campfire. A guitar is light, portable, and people like singing along. All you need to do is learn how to play it.

Fortunately this is not difficult. The lovely thing about the guitar is that it responds beautifully and immediately to whatever musicianship you put into it. It takes weeks just to get a decent note out of a flute or a violin, but you can wrest a damn good tune from a guitar just by playing the top string. Picking up a chord or two can be done in an afternoon. For even faster results, turn the pegs to produce what's called 'open tuning', where the guitar will play a chord without you putting your fingers on the frets. Then you can use a slide (a piece of metal or plastic that goes over the finger) to go up and down the frets, and wherever you land, it produces a perfect chord. It's cheating, but it sounds fantastic, like you've lived in the Mississippi Delta all your life. Ry Cooder does it – so why shouldn't you? And for additional effects you can use the use the body of the guitar as a percussion instrument.

If you find it hard to believe you can pick up guitar-playing in a couple of hours, give it a go. I promise it's not hard. Add friends and sunshine and you've got the ideal way to spend a summer's day.

57.

BUILD A TREEHOUSE

Building a treehouse is a job for someone who knows what they're doing. There's the matter of gravity, and what it does to bones. That said, it's a great summer project.

If you want to have a go, take some time choosing your location. Consider building between two or three trees rather than within a single tree: this is better for stability. If the trees are slender and in an exposed place they will move a fair bit in the wind. You can plan for this by using slots in the timber to allow movement, or by incorporating sliding beams. Consider carefully how high you want your treehouse. Just over an adult's head height is good for small children; higher is more exciting but the wind movement will be greater the higher you go.

Much of the treehouse, such as the walls and roof, can be prefabricated on the ground and assembled in the tree: you'll need, of course, a good cordless drill or a power supply with a long extension. At some point, you're going to need to drill into the tree to fix your arboreal home firmly into place. This won't harm the tree, though you should leave some space around your fixings for the tree to grow (trees grow by adding rings, so once they have reached a mature height they don't grow up but out).

A well-made treehouse should last for many summers, allowing much taking of secret oaths, much midnight feasting, much playing of guitars. Get some good plans, good tools and a good treehouse-building book. This isn't it!

58.

RUN A LEMONADE STAND (FOR CHARITY)

When life hands you lemons, make lemonade. And when you've made your lemonade, you can sell it.

Lemonade stands are a great way for kids to make money in summer. Adults can do it too. Why not? Especially if it's for a good cause.

Firstly, you'll need lemons. Real lemons, not powdered ones. Slice them, juice them, and put the juice and pulp in a pitcher with some water. Add plenty of sugar and some ice. Et *voilà*!

Secondly you'll need an eye-catching stand. A banner reading 'Lemonade for sale' has the twin advantages of brevity and clarity, and don't forget to give an indication of price – 50p per cup, perhaps. (Have plenty of paper cups, unless you're going truly up-market and offering it in wine-glasses.) If you're raising money for charity, make sure the name of the charity is prominent.

The location of your stand will determine how much you sell, so busy thoroughfares with lots of pedestrians are good. Make sure your stand is neat and tidy and that you are demure and respectful. Anyone who works in the food industry shouldn't look as if they've been rolling in germs.

Fourthly you'll need a hot day. You can capitalize on people's thirst by offering bottled water too. Make a big display of your bottled water and people will buy it to consume later.

Lastly, be a good salesperson. Offer refills for half price, lots of ice (keep it in a cooler), snacks and banter. Oh, and have a tip jar handy.

59.

HAVE A WATER-GUN FIGHT

A water-gun fight is an essential summer activity. Here's some ideas:

Fight in teams. Divide into equal groups and stage a war game. After a set period of time, the wettest team, as judged by an impartial observer, loses and gets profoundly drenched as a punishment.

Set the boundaries. Establish no-go areas: inside the house or near high-voltage electrical equipment are obvious ones.

Get a decent weapon. Pistols are peachy, but a blaster is faster. You can even get blasters with back-packs full of water to reduce the need to break and reload.

Have a filling station: running hoses or swimming pools are good. Make the filling station into a 'safe' area so that people re-filling can't be soaked while they are vulnerable.

Use water balloons. Balloons are the grenades of the water fight. Make lots in advance and when you've finished fighting, play games with them, such as a racing in pairs with a water balloon poised between the backs of each pair. Or try splitting into teams and launching water balloons at the opposing team with towels. If the opposing team an catch the balloon in their towel without it breaking, they win; if they get drenched, they lose.

Have water gun duels. Start back to back, take ten paces forward, turn and fight to the death.

Please invite me.

60.

WORSHIP THE SUN

It's difficult to argue with an Aztec. Any rational observer, starting from first principles, would conclude that the sun is the greatest of the gods. The sun bathes the planet with its heat and light, powers the weather, the seasons, and life itself, is so vast that a million earths could fit inside it, has storms so dreadful that they could obliterate worlds, and yet is so gentle – so forbearing, one might say – that a child in a pram can reach for it as its first toy. Its arrival in the morning and departure at evening hold an inexhaustible fascination. To see the sun poised on the rim of the world, a ball resting miraculously on a fence, is to be presented with a profound mystery. Where do the days go? Where will we be when another one is over? What countless ancestors have stood still at sunrise, groping wordlessly for meaning, and watched the clouds whispering together like a congregation waiting for a bishop?

If a new religion for the twenty-first century is to arise, in short, it should focus on the entity that lies at the basis of being. In this new religion, sunrise and sunset would be sacred, and so everyone would get up early. Solar power would be developed as a religious duty, and so the world's energy needs would be solved. The ziggurat would return as an architectural form. Only this time, stone knives would be less in evidence.

61.

DRAW ON THE PAVEMENT WITH COLOURED CHALKS

Summer is a great time for pavement art. It's less likely to be raining and people are in less of a hurry: they might even throw money your way. In recent years public chalk art has really taken off in popularity, thanks mainly to the new vogue for anamorphic street art. This is two-dimensional art that gives an illusion of three dimensions when viewed from a particular angle, conjuring up waterfalls disappearing into apparently solid ground or dinosaurs rearing through shattered flagstones.

Naturally you don't have to go all out and plan one of these: you can have a go with something inspired by your favourite painting, or by graffiti or cartoon characters. Just make sure you find out which parts of your town or city are zoned for street art: most authorities take a tolerant view as long as the chalks can be washed off by rain (don't use oil pastels!). There are now many festivals worldwide devoted to pavement art, among them the Imadon Festival in London's Covent Garden and the Sarasota Chalk Festival in Florida.

For kids, chalk can be a lot of fun. They can draw treasure maps. Or family portraits. They can play noughts and crosses, hangman or darts (where you draw the board and then play with small stones). They can draw a rainbow with a leprechaun at the end. They can make up a board game where they themselves are the pieces. They can make a race track for toy cars. Hopscotch is only the beginning.

62.

RENT A BEACH HUT

Beach huts have become something of a fetish in some quarters. They're just one-room sheds, yet in recent years they have come to command ever-higher prices. The record for the most expensive beach hut ever is £216,000 in 2006. Admittedly this was a luxury shed with mains electricity and running water where the owner could stay overnight, and with spectacular views over Chesil Beach.

Beach huts evolved from the bathing machines of the Victorian era. Bathing machines were horse-drawn wheeled vehicles that allowed men and women to change their clothing and delivered them decorously to the waves. By the Edwardian era, bathing machines had gone out of fashion and were being replaced by stationary huts that did the same job. At first, these were little more than holiday hutches for the labouring masses, who rented them on a daily or weekly basis at resorts such as Skegness or Blackpool, but in the 1970s and 1980s they increasingly came under private ownership. They are now often now looked on as cultural treasures. The UK is probably the most hutophiliac of all nations (there are around 20,000 country-wide), but there are large pockets of obsession in countries such as Australia, France and South Africa.

Why are beach huts so attractive, and why should you rent one? The appeal of the beach hut is probably related to the appeal of the garden shed. It's a place to meditate, to read the paper, to brew tea, to reflect on the follies of the world, and, especially in Britain, to escape from the rain. Ah, summer!

63.

CREATE AN IKEBANA DISPLAY

Ikebana is the ancient Japanese art of flower and foliage arrangement. You will need not merely flowers but also leaves, twigs, bark, branches, grasses and imagination.

First, you should forget what you know about Western flower display. In the Western tradition, displays are usually symmetrical, featuring closely-packed elements, and are very colourful, focussing on a balance of flower hues. Ikebana is just the opposite. It is usually asymmetrical, with few elements, and with only sparse and irregular distribution of colour. It also has an important cultural and spiritual dimension. Some ikebana displays have three elements: sky, humanity and earth. Plants found in the mountains are incorporated in the sky section, and point upwards; plants in lowland areas are placed in the humanity section of the display, and point outwards, and plants from ground level are in the earth section, and point downwards. Other methods focus on symbols of the sun, moon and earth. The container for the flowers is important too. Traditional fired pots are commonly used, but in modern ikebana one can also see imaginative uses of dishes, birds-nests, sculptural forms or even lengths of rusty steel tubing.

Ikebana was first developed by Japanese monks, and some schools of ikebana have a strong masculine flavour. Many ikebana flower displays don't have any flowers at all.

64.

WATCH GLOW-WORMS

Glow-worms are also known as fireflies or lightning bugs. There are many species, some winged and some wingless, but they all belong to the family *Lampyridae*, and are all beetles. They range over the world and can be found in a wide range of habitats, though given the choice you might be better off looking in isolated areas away from man-made lights and near water. Woodland, grassland or marshland would be good spots.

Glow-worms have been a source of fascination since the earliest written records: they are mentioned in Chinese documents from the first millennium BC, and make a fleeting appearance in *Hamlet* ('The glow worm shows the matin to be near/And 'gins to pale his uneffectual fire.') They produce light through a phenomenon called bioluminescence, which is a chemical reaction catalysed by an enzyme known as luciferase. ('Lucifer' is the 'light-bringer' of the Bible.)

Glow-worms emit pulses of light to send messages about food and reproductive health; and when two glow worms are on the same wavelength they begin to pulse in synchrony with a flashing 'Christmas tree' effect.

Some species of glow-worms (there are dozens) are endangered, so it is not a good idea to catch them and keep them in a jar. Certainly you should not do what one country gentleman was reported to have done, which was to catch a number of glow-worms and put them in a bicycle light when his batteries failed.

65.

TIE-DYE A T-SHIRT

It's summer, so it's time to emulate the people who work in health shops. Tie-dyeing is a cheap way to look good, and it's fun.

First get a cotton t-shirt (you can tie-dye anything, even lingerie, but its best to start with a t-shirt) and use rubber bands or string to tie off sections of it. You can do this in a completely free-form way – the result will be largely unpredictable – or you can go for a more measured approach. A spiral is probably the easiest symmetrical design: for this, pinch up the fabric in the middle of the t-shirt and twist it until the t-shirt forms a circular wad. Then tie it tightly into place.

Next, the dyeing. For best results use fibre-reactive dyes. These can be found in craft shops, and will ensure that your design doesn't fade after the first wash. (For even better results, soak the t-shirt in sodium carbonate beforehand: this will allow the dye to bond even more permanently with the fabric.) Donning your rubber gloves, dip the bound t-shirt into a bucket of dye for a few minutes, then remove it and leave it to dry. Repeat for subsequent colours (go from the lightest colour to the darkest). For a less muddy and more colourful approach, don't dip. Instead use squeezy bottles of dye to apply colour to different sections of the t-shirt. These bottles can also be bought in craft shops.

Leave overnight, remove the ties and rinse thoroughly. Add peace jewellery and guitar.

66.

BUILD A WICKER MAN

Effigies of men have been constructed and burned throughout history. Sometimes they have been large enough to accommodate human sacrifices. Julius Caesar in his *Gallic Wars* mentioned that the Druids executed prisoners in this way. Suetonius in *The Twelve Caesars* also described German tribesmen burning Roman captives alive in gigantic wicker cages. The modern image of the practice is probably influenced by the 1973 horror film *The Wicker Man* (remade in 2006 with Nicholas – appropriately – Cage), in which a policeman is immolated by some very single-minded villagers. Its greatest apotheosis in modern times is in the Burning Man festival in the Black Rock Desert of Nevada, which annually attracts over 200,000 people and features pyrotechnics, massive sculptures, futuristic vehicles, eco-awareness and public nudity. The climax of the festival is the firing of a 40-metre-plus high wooden man (known as 'the Man') stuffed with neon tubes.

You may not be able to afford a ticket to Burning Man but you can create your own. You'll need first of all some sort of burning platform of slabs or rocks to avoid scarring the ground. Then a skeleton, fixed securely into the base: it's easiest to create this from wood. Then shape the man-sculpture using flexible twigs such as willow or alder. You can buy willow rods for the purpose quite cheaply online. Finally, sculpt a head from finer twigs and place it on top.

Stay your match-hand until some suitable occasion, such as the summer solstice.

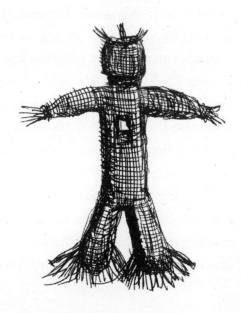

67.

MAKE SMOOTHIES

Making smoothies is the closest most people get to alchemy: working with the contents of the kitchen, you become a latter-day Paracelsus, seeking to transmute base foodstuffs into gold.

First you need fruit. Anything is fine, though some fruits will result in a thicker smoothie than others. Bananas, peaches, apricots, strawberries and avocados will give a thick smoothie, whereas oranges, pineapples, watermelon and other juicier fruits will tend towards a thinner concoction.

Secondly you need some sort of liquid foundation. Water is fine, but you can also use milk, yoghurt, fruit juice or tea (to take the edge off the sweetness).

Now flavourings. What about cinnamon or honey? Or nutmeg and vanilla extract? A heavy hand with these can lead to the whole thing being poured down the sink (along with a pound of expensive strawberries), so try to keep your enthusiasm from spilling over.

Next, some summer cooling. Ice-cream is delicious in a smoothie; you can also add ice-cubes to the mix. When you have all your ingredients in the blender, give it a good grind. The result might be ridiculous or delicious. For an example of the latter, try this: a peanut butter smoothie. Take a half cup of peanut butter, three scoops of ice-cream, two cups of milk, a banana and two tablespoons of honey. Blend and leave to settle. Garnish with chopped almonds. Serves two.

68.

MAKE ICE-CREAM

Ice-cream is surprisingly easy to make. You don't need a large stainless-steel machine, or your own cow. You just need the following:

4 egg yolks

a teaspoon of cornflour

3 ½ oz (100g) caster sugar

½ pint (300ml) double cream

½ pint (300ml) full fat milk

a vanilla pod or a half teaspoon of vanilla essence

Mix the egg yolks with the caster sugar, cornflour and vanilla essence (or the seeds of the vanilla pod), stirring until you have a smooth paste. Then mix the cream and milk in a saucepan and bring to just below boiling. Stir in the egg mixture, a little at a time. Simmer for ten minutes, stirring all the time. Then transfer to a freezer-proof container and leave to acquire room temperature. When cool, transfer to the fridge and leave overnight. The next day, freeze the mixture for an hour. Take it out after this time and whisk to disperse the ice crystals. Replace in the freezer for another hour and then repeat the process. Repeat for a third and final time before leaving the ice-cream to freeze solid.

Naturally you can add other flavours (after the mixture is cool). Fresh strawberries, honey and cinnamon, Earl Grey tea: anything that you think will cause people to open their mouths with astonishment. And people very easily open their mouths with astonishment when presented with home-made ice-cream.

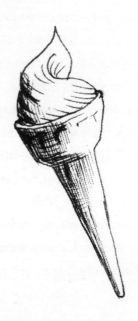

69.

HAVE A GARAGE SALE

Most people's houses are full of piles of junk they don't need, and are often lacking in piles of cash they do need. With that in mind, why not try a garage sale? Here are some ways to make it a success.

Advertise the sale well beforehand. You might want to consider an ad in a local newspaper. Certainly put up signs in the locality directing people to the sale (with arrows for half a mile around); make sure you take the signs down afterwards.

Choose a good day. A weekend is best: you may wish to run the sale over a Saturday and a Sunday for maximum returns. If the weather is foul, cancel it and re-schedule. No one will come to a garage sale when it's bucketing down.

Make sure everything is (i) attractively presented, preferably on tables, and (ii) clearly priced. Clear pricing reduces the need to haggle and makes sales faster.

Don't be tempted to overprice items. People coming to a garage sale are looking for bargains, and won't appreciate being asked to pay the same price as they would in a shop.

Look after your cash. A cash-box or midriff wallet is a good option. Make sure you've got lots of spare change on the morning of the sale. Assigning someone the specific role of cashier helps.

Reduce prices at the end of the sale to clear the remaining stock. Of those things that remain, advertise them on Freecycle.

Finally, if you don't have a garage or a garden or any large open area in front of your house, approach anyone nearby who does, and have a multi-family garage sale. This will bring in more customers and generate a nice community atmosphere.

70.

MAKE A DAISY CHAIN

The world's longest daisy chain was 125½ yards long and was created by Erin, Robert, Sasha, Meng-wei, Polly and Agatha in Leek, Staffordshire on the 14th August 2007. It involved 4,894 daisies plucked from the surrounding countryside, and in fact led to a virtual eradication of daisies from Leek for the duration of the summer. The record-breaking chain itself is still in cold storage at Polly's mum's house in a Quality Street tin in the freezer.

While activity on this gargantuan scale should probably not be encouraged, making smaller daisy chains is a fun thing to do on a summer's day. You can make daisy necklaces, daisy headbands, daisy anklets and wristlets. Even daisy legwarmers. All you need is a good supply of daisies and a strong thumbnail. Stocky daisies with thick stems are the best: split each daisy stalk with your thumbnail about halfway down and insert the head of the next daisy into the hole, continuing until you have the required length. Then, to form a circle, simply insert the head of the first daisy into the stalk of the last.

Daisy-chain-making is a great summer activity for kids, because even the youngest child can master the technique and take pride in the results.

71.

ORGANIZE A FROG-JUMPING COMPETITION

Frog-jumping really starts with a short story by Mark Twain, 'The Celebrated Jumping Frog of Calaveras County', published in 1865. This recounts an episode in which two frog-fanciers pit their long-jumping frogs against one another, but things turn nasty when one fancier secretly pours lead shot into his competitor's frog's gullet and immobilizes it. The story was an enormous hit and led to the establishment of frog-jumping competitions all over the United States and beyond.

In Angels Camp, California, where the original story was set, over 3,000 frogs compete annually. The frogs are placed (or dropped, actually, to stimulate them) on a starting spot and then encouraged to jump towards a perimeter. If they make the perimeter within three jumps the total distance is measured and a prize awarded to the furthest-flung. Participants must not touch their frogs to make them jump, but screaming, pounding the ground and otherwise terrifying the amphibians into an early grave are encouraged. The best effort recorded was by Rosie the Ribeter in 1986, and measured 21 feet 5¾ inches. At Angels Camp there is a $5000 prize to any frog that can beat this record.

Some competitions are more soliticious of amphibian welfare than others, and mandate the playing of soothing music in the frog paddock before the jump-off.

Frogs abound in summer. Why not start a competition?

72.

GO SNAIL-RACING

Snail racing is rather similar to frog-jumping, except that the action takes place over longer periods of time.

Snail-racing can be enjoyed at numerous country fairs. The race starts by placing all the snails on a spot at the centre of a large circle. The perimeter of the circle is dotted with tasty pieces of greenery: snails are particularly ravenous for the leaves of sunflowers or beans (as gardeners know well). At a signal of 'On your marks, get set, slime!' the race begins. And so the long day wears on. Eventually a snail might leave the central spot to see what's happening and if there's anything to eat. The pack of snails gradually fans out, idly approaching the perimeter, or thinking better of it, doubling back and falling asleep. Meanwhile the spectators steadily approach the acme of their snail-frenzy, screaming the names of their favourites, staking and raising bets, beckoning them with tasty treats. Finally a snail, more out of luck than judgement, makes the perimeter: a klaxon is sounded and there are wild cheers. The race is over. The losing snails are taken up, scolded, and threatened with a salt bath unless they do better next time. There is no empty commiseration in this most Darwinian of struggles.

Slug-racing is a variant on snail-racing, but to the present author's knowledge no professional meets have ever been held.

73.

DO SOME HOG CALLING

Hog calling is a competitive sport that doesn't involve hogs. It is done at county fairs and on other bucolic occasions, and no accessories are required. The contestants usually perform on a stage with a microphone.

The purpose is ostensibly to 'call' the hog, but since no hogs are present to prick up their ears and come trotting over to a bowl of swill, the contestants are required to satisfy other criteria, the chief one of which seems to be to be entertaining. There are several common components: long skirling or whooping calls of 'Soooooooieee!', repetitive chants of 'here piggypiggypiggypiggy' and actual imitations of the grunts, squeals and feeding behaviour of pigs. William Hedgepeth has written the definitive guide to the subject, *The Hog Book*, and says that 'Soooooooieee!' is the most common noise but that 'Hooooooieee!' is a common vairiant. This latter seems to have been the approach taken up by PG Wodehouse in his Blandings Castle short story 'Pig-hoo-o-o-o-ey', in which Lord Emsworth's pig, the Empress of Blandings, goes off her swill after the departure of his Lordship's pigman, and is only persuaded to eat when a visitor from Nebraska advises his Lordship that the 'master-call' for pigs is 'Pig-hoo-o-o-o-ey!'

So if you have the lungs and the nerve, have a go this summer. If you can't find a contest, start your own. No qualifications are necessary except the ability to produce, as Hedgepeth says, 'a plorative unleashing of richest animal volume, a supersonic hog call whose sheer piercing magnitude can break glass, puncture tires, separate tissue; a beckoning love song to swine yet unborn.'

74.

IDENTIFY WILD FLOWERS

Flower-spotting has an advantage over bird-spotting: flowers stay still, whereas birds do not. If you're in doubt as to what a flower is, you can always go back the next day with a book, or take a photograph; it will probably be there when you return.

Flower identification, with the help of a good handbook, is rarely difficult, but a cursory knowledge of flower anatomy is helpful. Sepals lie at the base of the flower and enclose it; petals are the brightly-coloured outgrowths that attract animals (flowers are 'tarts for the bees' as Uncle Monty put it in *Withnail and I*); stamens are filaments tipped with pollen; stigmas are the sticky receptors of pollen; and the style supports the stigma, rather like a bench of magistrates. These and other anatomical features are often notated using abbreviations, so that, for experts, flower identification can look something like maths: the floral formula for the geranium, for example, is $Ca^5CoZ^5A^6G(5)^{superior}$.

One thing to stress is that if in doubt about a flower identification, don't pick it to show to someone or for ease of reference later on. The rule is 'Bring the book to the plant, not the plant to the book.' If you don't have a camera, make a sketch, and note details of the size, leaf-shape, colour of flowers, arrangement of flowers on the stalk, habitat, abundance, degree of hairiness and other anatomical details.

Wild flower identification is in some ways the perfect summer hobby: it requires no equipment or athletic ability and is inexhaustibly fascinating; and when you've finished with the wild flowers of your own country, you can graduate to the world's.

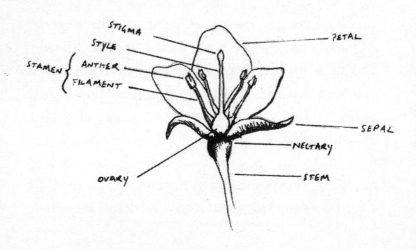

75.

IDENTIFY TREES

'The trees are coming into leaf, like something
almost being said.'
Philip Larkin, 'The Trees'

In summer the full beauty of trees can be appreciated.
A mature oak or copper beech at the height of the
season, its great mass of foliage stirring in the wind,
is a magnificent spectacle; then again so is a single
spare Scots Pine, clinging to a ragged hillside, or a
perplexing monkey-puzzle. Trees have been called the
lungs of the planet. That may be true, but even more
so they are the conscience of the planet. A society that
loves trees lives in symbiosis with nature and respects
it. Trees that are ill-treated die, and leave us with
nothing but concrete. They are vast but vulnerable.
They can't run away from pollution or a chainsaw.
The degree to which we treat them well is the degree

to which we can restrain our immediate impulses, cherish what is beautiful and think of the future.

Is an ability to identify trees a moral duty, therefore? Certainly not. It's fun! Get a good handbook and go out for a walk. As with learning a foreign language, you will feel yourself to be a genius within the first half hour. But unlike learning a foreign language, the feeling that you are a genius doesn't wear off. Suddenly you have a hobby that can be indulged in wherever you go. Soon you will throw the book away, and all you will need are the leaves, flowers, fruits and bark.

76.

DON'T PLANT A TREE

Summer is the perfect time not to plant a tree. This may seem a strange thing to say. But you should at least think very carefully before planting a tree. The reasons are twofold.

Firstly, just because a habitat doesn't have a tree doesn't mean that it needs one. A habitat might be functioning very well – might exist in a perfect balance of plants, insects and other wildlife – without trees. The introduction of trees might threaten a much rarer habitat.

Secondly, there is a risk of disease. The scourge of Ash Dieback in European forests is due to the import of ash trees within European member states, but this is only the most recent manifestation of the problems that can be caused by imported specimens. Previous to Ash Dieback, there was Dutch Elm Disease, then Sudden Oak Death, then fungal diseases affecting willows and alders. We now face the globalization of tree diseases.

Trees are very good at planting themselves without any help from us. And a wood is a very different thing from a plantation. In a wood you have trees of different ages, of different species, in different proportions. If we value trees, we should be looking far more cleverly at the natural regeneration of woodlands.

The UK and other European countries are pretty well served for trees. There are probably more trees in Britain at the moment than at any time since the medieval period. We should cherish the ones we have and protect them. But planting new ones might conceivably endanger the ones we are already lucky enough to have.

77.

OBSERVE THE WILL O' THE WISP

How often do you get the chance to observe a genuinely unexplained natural phenomenon? For that's what the will o' the wisp is. Many cultures around the world have stories attesting to a bluish light that hovers over marshy ground, only to recede when observers try to get near it. Legends tell of a sprite or pixy, exiled from hell or heaven, who is forced to wander the earth with a glowing lamp, hoping to lure travellers to their deaths in the bog. Japan, Russia, Finland, Ireland, America all have their will o' the wisp stories: in Scandinavian legend the phenomenon is particularly associated with summer, because the goblin who wields the unearthly fire has buried a treasure that can only be dug up in the summer months.

Science (which has dubbed it *ignis fatuus*, or foolish

fire) remains baffled as to the exact nature of the will o' the wisp. One guess is that it is produced by methane emanating from swampy land, which is then ignited by lightning; other theories involve the discharge of geo-electricity under tectonic strain (though none of these theories explains why the will o' the wisp appears to recede when approached).

The best places to observe the will o' the wisp is in wet ground with lots of superstitious folk around.

78.

HOLD A LUAU

Tired of ordinary garden parties? Then why not hold a luau? A luau is a a traditional Hawaiian party. For a luau, you need the right food, the right clothes, the right music and the right atmosphere.

The right food is Hawaiian food, obviously, which is heavy on pork and seafood. The pork should be roasted (see §79, BBQ a pig); and for seafood, use limpets (called *opihi* in Hawaii), lomi salmon (salmon and tomato, served cold) or octopus. Mashed taro root, called *poi*, can also be served, if you can get hold of any. As for clothes, you can't go wrong with colourful flower-pattern shirts and dresses, and of course *lei*, or flower garlands. The right music is achieved by hiring traditional Hawaiian musicians at enormous expense, or alternatively with a CD of Hawaiian music. And the right atmosphere (very important!) is achieved by copious servings of *mai tai*, a traditional Hawaian cocktail composed of white rum, dark rum, curacao and lime juice with a piece of pineapple for garnish. This magically engenders a Hawaiian atmosphere within a radius of 100 yards.

A Hawaiian food fight is sometimes called 'the king of food fights' because of the prevalence of octopus and limpets, the shells of which can cause nasty cuts. Only an Icelandic food fight, in which fermented shark is employed, is more spectacular.

79.

BBQ A PIG

A barbecue is a mini-spectacle, a theatre of food, utilizing fire, smoke, raw meat and sweat; and no more so than when whole animals are being cooked.

So for a real barbecue you need a pig. You could barbecue a whole lamb or whole chicken (see §81, Hangi a chicken) but a pig makes the most impact, mainly because it *looks* so whole, with its head on and everything. Some BBQ-ers will roast a pig and eat the brains, but perhaps it's better to gloss over that.

So, how to do it? A suckling pig is best (somewhere between 20-30 lbs), because the meat is tenderer and the size of it is more manageable: for this we're talking about a pig somewhere around six weeks old (after which they start going indoors for rearing up to wiener weight).

Marinading beforehand is optional; some sort of oil-based marinade will help the cooking. The pig can be stuffed and sewn up if preferred. You will probably need some sort of spit mechanism, either electric or hand-turned, though pigs can be barbecued just by placing them on a slow grill, ideally one with a closed cover. Use charcoal or wood, the more aromatic the wood the better. Don't use household wood scraps and offcuts because these may contain paint and preservative chemicals that will taint the meat. You can use a gas or electric grill of course, though surely that reduces some of the point of having a barbecue in the first place.

Serve with coleslaw, baked potatoes, beans, salad.

80.

HAVE A KEG-A-QUE

Having advised readers to barbecue a pig, it occurs that some might not own a barbecue. Well, this problem is very simply and cheaply remedied. You can spend an enjoyable summer's day making your own barbecue.

The only real requirement is that you build your barbecue out of something non-combustible – such as stone or metal. There are a wide variety of options to choose from. For example, you could have a keg-a-que. This involves finding an old metal beer keg (the type that are about two to three feet high), cutting it in half lengthways with an angle grinder, and using the interior of the keg to build a fire. Lay a grill on top and you have a very serviceable barbecue. Or you can do the same thing with an old oil drum: by the time you've finished you will have enough grill space to feed a wedding party. An old car wheel rim can also serve as a small barbecue.

A stone barbecue is probably the easiest of all to make. Simply find enough stone blocks or bricks and arrange them in a circular stack. Light a fire inside and put a grill on top. The gaps between the bricks provide plenty of good airflow to keep the fire going (if you opt for a metal barbecue you may find that you have to drill holes to increase airflow).

In short, don't buy a barbecue and have it hanging around dismally all winter. Make one yourself at a fraction of the price – from stuff that was hanging around already.

81.

HANGI A CHICKEN

A 'hangi' is a traditional Maori method of cooking using hot rocks or hot irons. It makes an interesting alternative to a barbecue, and there's an element of magic to it, because it involves cooking underground.

What you need is a whole dressed chicken, some large rocks or large pieces of iron (as big as the palm of your hand), some hessian sacking, some tin foil and some cabbage leaves (a couple of cabbages should do it).

First, dig a pit in the ground about two feet deep. Then heat up your rocks or irons. The best way to do this is simply to have a bonfire and keep the rocks or irons in the hottest part of the bonfire for about two hours. When the fire has burnt down, drag out the hot rocks or irons and place them in the bottom of the hole. Throw the cabbage leaves on top: this will generate a lot of steam, which will help to cook the meat. The chicken, wrapped in cabbage leaves and foil, goes on top of the rocks; you can also add potatoes or apples as side dishes or to give more flavour to the chicken itself. Wet hessian sacks are placed on top of the chicken. Finally, the whole thing is covered with earth.

After three to four hours you can remove the earth and retrieve the chicken, which will be done to a turn, tender and aromatic. If you don't tell anyone what you're doing beforehand, it will be quite a surprise when you excavate their dinner.

82.

GO TO AN OUTDOOR FILM SCREENING

For film buffs, summer offers an unparalleled pleasure: the opportunity to see movies on the big screen while zephyrs caress your half-clothed limbs and the moon shines down from above. In the UK, some of the best screens are in London (the enormous screen in the Fountain Square at Somerset House, or the Open Air Cinema at Kensington Palace, for example). Versatile promoters now show also films in locations such as rooftops, pubs, car parks and gardens.

Of course, the epitome of the outdoor experience is the drive-in. You sit simultaneously inside and outside, while the soundtrack is piped to your car radio, and get on with whatever extracurricular activities you have in mind, perhaps even ignoring the movie entirely. For the authentic '50s experience you should probably sit on top of the car, preferably one with fins, and hurl popcorn into the projector beam.

A modern take on the outdoor movie is the 'guerrilla' al fresco screening. These can be organised with modern equipment such as LCD projectors; the screens can be anything from the sides of buildings to the archways of motorway bridges. Patrons are told about the screening by email or SMS just a few hours in advance, to avoid the cops.

83.

VISIT THE SUMMER EXHIBITION

The Royal Academy Summer Exhibition, held at Burlington House in Piccadilly, London, from June to August, was founded in 1769 as 'an annual exhibition open to all artists of distinguished merit'. It has been held every year since, and is the most popular open art exhibition in the UK.

The Summer Exhibition now shows work from a wide range of artists throughout the world. Anyone can apply – all ages and nationalities, trained or untrained – and the competition is fierce: of over 10,000 paintings, prints, sculptures and other works submitted annually, only about 1,000 make it into the galleries. Artists can submit up to two works each, and the fee for submissions (currently £25 each) goes toward the upkeep of the Royal Academy, which recieves no public grants. All works are for sale, so there is a chance for visitors to pick up a good investment.

The Summer exhibition has often been the focus of scandal. In 1850 the painting *Christ in the House of his Parents* by Millais drew condemnation from from all sides: *The Times* said it was 'plainly revolting' and Dickens wrote that the eight-year-old Christ in the picture was 'a hideous, wry-necked, blubbering, red-haired boy in a nightgown'. And in 1914 a Suffragette used a meat cleaver to attack John Singer Sargent's portrait of Henry James, severely damaging it. The Secretary of the Royal academy, Walter Lamb, commented at the time that 'in future artists will require to paint their pictures on armour plate'.

84.

GO TO THE OPERA – OUTDOORS

Listening to an opera outside is very different experience from being imprisoned in a plush seat and straining with your opera glasses. Hearing the music wafted to you on the breeze as you recline comfortably on the grass, your picnic lunch spread out in front of you and a glass of something bubbling in your hand, is possibly one of the most civilizing experiences of the 21st century. Consider a festival such as the West Green House Opera Festival in Hampshire. It's held at a beautiful English country house with extensive gardens near Farnborough, and is known for outdoor renderings of crowd-pleasers such as *The Tales of Hoffmann* or *The Threepenny Opera*. Or Glyndebourne near Lewes in Sussex, which focuses particularly on the operas of Mozart but also features works by composers as diverse as Gershwin and Janáček. You might have to have to dress up for it (sober suits for men and flowery dresses for ladies), but don't let that put you off. And for lovers of orchestral music, there's Kenwood House in London, which stages outdoor orchestral concerts throughout the summer months. Look out for the classic Kenwood House performance of the 1812 Overture by Tchaikovsky, complete with fireworks.

If you don't do it for the music, just do it for the picnic and the dresses!

85.

COMMEMORATE BLOOMSDAY

Bloomsday, one of the first cultural events of Summer, is held every year on June 16th. It commemorates the events of James Joyce's novel *Ulysses*, which all take place in Dublin on that single June day, originally in 1904. 'Bloomsday' is named after Leopold Bloom, the central figure of the novel.

Despite being deeply complex and in parts frankly impenetrable, *Ulysses* inspires fierce love and loyalty from fans around the world. In Dublin, Joyceophiles dress up in Edwardian finery and parade around the city, visiting various locations mentioned in the book and eating delicacies including 'the inner organs of beasts and fowls'.

The celebrations (often riotous and alcoholic) are not confined to Dublin. There are parallel celebrations in Trieste, Italy, where Joyce wrote much of the book, as well as in London, New York and Szombatheley,

Hungary, the hometown of the fictional Leopold Bloom's father, Rudolf Virag. (This is not the only instance of a festival dedicated to a fictional character, but must be the only festival dedicated to someone mentioned merely in passing in a 900-page book.)

In fact, wherever you are, there is likely to be a Bloomsday celebration going on somewhere: your library, perhaps, or the local radio station. The best way to celebrate might be to pick up a copy of *Ulysses* and attempt to read it.

86.

PLAY NIGHT TENNIS

The idea of playing tennis at night is not exactly new. That's what floodlights are for, after all. But real night tennis involves playing tennis in the dark.

Imagine: it's a sultry summer night, the court is marked out with fluorescent lines, and the net glows softly. The ball is day-glo and the players wear fluorescent outfits and wield fluorescent rackets. Day-glo spectators cheer as ghostly serves, rallies and smashes light up the gloom.

Good eyes and fast reactions are as important as (or more important than) in conventional tennis, though the matches tend to be shorter and there is more swearing.

It's been tried out all over the world and it has a following especially among younger people. After a good hard night's tennis, the net and umpire's perch can be cleared away and the court can turn into a disco.

Strawberries and cream are not generally in evidence since strawberries do not tend to promote good vision. Carrots and cream are the obvious alternative.

What next? Perhaps night dressage or night javelin (though perhaps not).

87.

PLAY ULTIMATE

Frisbee is a fun summer beach game, but for serious players, there is 'Ultimate'. 'Ultimate' was formerly called 'Ultimate Frisbee', but Frisbee is a trademark, and for that reason it was dropped; some players refer to the game as 'Flying Disc' or 'Ultimate Flying Disc'.

The rules are rather like basketball, only with no baskets (or ball). Two opposing teams, usually of seven players, attempt to pass the frisbee to one another so that they occupy the opposing team's home area, or 'end zone'. Play begins as each team lines up on the forward boundary of their end zone and the defence throws the Frisbee to the opposing team. The opposing team catch the Frisbee and try to make it towards their end zone. Once a successful pass has been completed in the end zone, the team wins a point and the direction of play is reversed. Passes may only be made while a player is stationary or pivoting on one leg; if any player runs with the Frisbee, it is a foul. Nor can any player hold on to the Frisbee for too long: an opposing player acting as a 'mark' counts loudly (and annoyingly) up to ten, after which, if the holder of the Frisbee hasn't thrown, he loses a point.

The word 'Frisbee' has an interesting history. The original Frisbees were tin pie plates made by the Frisbie pie company during the Second World War. The truck drivers experimented with throwing the tins and the game soon caught on among American soldiers.

88.

PLAY GAMES IN THE POOL

A visit to the pool is fun, but pool games make it even better.

Marco Polo is an aquatic version of Blind Man's Buff, for two to a dozen people. The rules are simple: the player who is 'It' is blindfolded. This player then shouts out 'Marco' and the other players must reply 'Polo'. The 'It' player then has to swim towards the others, relying on their responses to locate and catch them. The caught player then becomes 'It' and the game starts again. If the 'It' player suspects a player has left the pool to elude them, they may shout 'on the rocks!', and if it's a fair cop, the player who has left the pool takes their place. (In a variant, a shout of 'mermaid on the rocks!' indicates that someone is sitting on the edge of the pool dipping their legs in).

Or try Sharks and Minnows. This is a pool version of 'bulldog' for as many people as possible. The 'shark' is stationed in the middle of the pool, facing the deep end. At a given signal, the minnows, lined up at the deep end, dive in and must swim past the shark to the shallow end without being tagged. If they make it, they survive until the next round, and if they are tagged they join the shark. This continues until all the minnows are caught. The game can also be played across the width of the pool to give the minnows more of a chance.

Or you can play pool football, pool cricket or pool rugby. In fact, whatever you can play out of a pool, you can usually play in it.

89.

GO SUMMER SLEDDING

Sledding without snow is not impossible. There are plenty of ways you can use the combination of a hill, gravity and a flat-bottomed vehicle to have fun. Here are a few:

Cardboarding. If the hill is steep and flat enough, a big piece of cardboard held up at the leading edge will provide you with a sled. Sounds crazy but it works.

Iceblocking. Buy a large piece of ice - available at some supermarkets or at specialist retailers who supply to the ice sculpture industry – lay a cloth on top of the ice, and ride the ice to perdition.

Wetsledding. If you have a water source near the hill, soak the hill and ride down it on anything with a flat bottom. Sled, teatray, etc. This also works if it's rained recently.

Mudsledding. Same thing, but with mud. Wear swimming costume and kneepads.

Plasticsledding. If you can find a big roll of flat plastic sheeting, lay it down the length of the hill. Get on a sled formed from a piece of the same plastic, and shoot down the hill. Totally frictionless!

Or if you're in Hollywood, borrow a snow-making machine…

90.

APPROXIMATE THE VALUE OF PI BY THROWING HOT DOGS

Summer is a great time to have a barbecue, as we've already seen. When the eating and drinking are over, you may still have some extra sausages left over. If you are feeling mathematically inclined, why not use them to calculate the value of pi?

The method is simplicity itself. Use long, thin sausages or hot dogs if possible. Then clear a throwing area about 10 feet (3m) long. Starting half-way up the throwing area, put down several 4 foot (1.3m) pieces of tape, spaced apart as far as your sausages are long, parallel to one another, and perpendicular to the direction of throw (so if your sausages are six inches (15cm) long, put the lengths of tape six inches apart, going laterally, like a height chart).

Now, standing at the back of the throwing area,

throw the hot dogs toward the tapes. Don't aim at any individual tape: just throw them towards the tapes. You will notice that some sausages land on the tapes, and some don't. If a sausage comes to rest touching a tape, mark it as a hit. Throw a couple of hundred times, noting the hits. Now comes the part where food becomes maths. Divide 2 by the number of hits, multiplied by the total number of throws. Thus, if you threw 250 sausages in all, and scored 159 times, the sum is (2/159) x 250.

You may be surprised by the results.

The sausages will be a little grubby by now, but they can easily be washed off and eaten. Perhaps in a pi...

91.

PICK YOUR OWN SEASONAL FRUITS

If you've never eaten a freshly picked stolen strawberry, you're either an honest person or a farmer.

As the summer months get into gear, pick-your-own farms appear throughout the countryside, and they are cheap! Much cheaper than the supermarkets. Pick-your-own farms often also have shops attached to them that sell all sorts of other local products that you can't get anywhere else – cheeses, meats, wines, yoghurts, chutneys and so on. They're a great way to support your local economy and your own economy.

People do tend to cheat a bit, of course. It seems to be part of the experience. The owners are obviously aware of what goes on, but seem to turn a blind eye to the punters (or punneters) popping the occasional fruit in their mouths. Owners even seem to welcome children – who might as well be coming in with a bowl of cream and a spoon, for all the genuine picking they do.

If, by the end of the day, you have eaten so much fruit that you can't stand the thought of another strawberry (or raspberry, redcurrant, etc) for the rest of your life, then try some jam-making or baking. Victoria sponge with fresh strawberries and whipped cream is an experience that should be – but happily isn't – reserved for humanity's heroes, such as those who broker world peace or eliminate deadly viruses.

92.

SPIT WATERMELON SEEDS

The idea here is to spit a mouthful of watermelon seeds as far as you can. The record is 68 feet 9 1/8 inches (20.95m) by Lee Wheelis in Luling, Texas, in 1989. A few commonly accepted rules:

Spitting can take place indoors or outdoors, but if outdoors, it should be a windless day.

Distance is usually recorded on a special roll-out mat; the seeds must land on the mat to count.

The total distance travelled includes the distance that the watermelon seed travels after it hits the floor.

A running start is acceptable.

The Watermelon Queen should stand 'up-spit'.

As the American National Watermelon Association puts it: 'Watermelon is healthy and nutritious for you and watermelon-spitting is part of Americana.' Fortunately watermelons are a global commodity and you can take part wherever you live.

93.

FORAGE FOR SEAWEED

It's the end of a perfect summer day at the seaside, and the lowering sun is glinting gently off the waves. The other holidaymakers are packing up their bags and preparing for an evening at the hotel bar. You, meanwhile, have just arrived with your bucket and a pair of scissors. You're here to get dinner.

Worldwide, there are about 10,000 types of seaweed, and, except in countries like Japan, it is strangely neglected as a food source. Seaweed is delicious and nutritious: it's a great source of sodium, iodine and antioxidants. The Welsh know it as laver, and make bread with it. Porridge can be flavoured with it. It can be shredded onto rice. And it makes a great salad ingredient.

With that in mind, paddle into the shallows at low tide. A good first candidate is sea-lettuce, which has long, green fronds that are almost translucent. Don't pull it off its anchoring-place on the rocks, simply snip off the tops with your scissors and put it in your bucket. (Never collect loose-floating seaweed, since it may not be fresh.) Next, search out some oarweed. This is brown, with thick stems and fronds that look like a hand with many long waving fingers. Then, if you are lucky enough to find it, gather samphire (also known as glasswort), which is delectable pickled or in salads and is mentioned in *King Lear*.

If you're unsure about which species is which, bring some pictures or a book to the beach with you. You will soon become an expert.

94.

CLEAN UP A BEACH

Unfortunately, amid the sea-lettuce and mussels on your local beach you are likely to find some rather more inedible items: cigarette butts, condoms, plastic bags, six-pack holders, sanitary pads and chocolate bar wrappers. These are not just unsightly, but a danger to wildlife: animals such as turtles or seals can be ensnared in plastic detritus or eat trash, with fatal consequences. And there is a threat to human health too: people can cut themselves on glass, or pick up infections.

Much of this rubbish is thrown or washed overboard by shipping (there's something called the Pacific Trash Vortex which is a thousand-square-mile patch of bobbing plastic ducks and training shoes), but the largest proportion comes from land-based sources: rubbish in our streets can be washed into storm drains and then out into the ocean, where it ends up on the beach, or it can be dumped by irresponsible parties or simply left behind by beachgoers.

What to do? Well, before you lay on a beach, give it a manicure. Join a beach rescue party in your local area. They'll advise you on the best places to start and what to look for, and will put you in touch with other like-minded spirits. You should wear good boots and sturdy gloves that will protect you against some of the more unsavoury aspects of beach-life.

If you live near a beach, this is self-protection: local economies depend on the health of their coastal environments for tourism, recreation and work. Dead animals and syringes are never good for business.

95.

SEE THE COALSACK

The Coalsack is a region of the night sky that is very dark against the surrounding stars. It's located at the southern end of the Milky Way.

Why go out and see the Coalsack? Well, if you can see the Coalsack at all, you will be somewhere very, very far away from light pollution. In the UK, the north of Norfolk or the north of Scotland are good places. And if you are somewhere very, very far away from light pollution, you will be able to see the rest of the stars, which are a magnificent spectacle. So to see the Coalsack – a region notable for having no stars (or very few that are visible to the naked eye) – is to be able to see the galaxy. And this is something very rare in modern life.

In Australian Aboriginal tradition, the dark patches in the sky – of which the Coalsack is the most prominent – are actually the most familiar and recognizable portions of the sky. In fact, the dark portions of the sky, rather than the stars, make up the constellations. That's how clear the skies are at night in Australia. The Coalsack, in some Aboriginal traditions, forms the head of a cosmic emu. It even has a small but identifiable beak.

96.

MAKE A MUDMAN

It's summer, so you can't make a snowman. The obvious solution is to make a mudman.

Mudmen are slightly more difficult to make than snowmen, because of the fact that mud weighs more, doesn't stick together as well as snow, and has a tendency to collapse under its own weight. For these reasons you need to make a solid skeleton for your mudman, and the best way to do this is to get a plastic bin. For a three foot high mudman (don't be too ambitious) get a two foot high pedal bin or wastebin. Fill it with a little mud for stability, and then plaster round it. If you insert spikes through the sides of the bin poking out at various widths you will have something for the plastered mud to stick onto. Then put an old basketball on top and plaster over that. A carrot for a nose and some coal for the eyes finishes the mudman off.

If you want to go all out and confuse people, you could spray your mudman with fake snow. Or, if you want your mudman to come to life, try mixing grass seeds in with the mud: mist your mudman regularly and you will have a turfman.

97.

BEGIN WRITING AN EROTIC NOVEL

Human beings do not come into oestrus, so there is no reason why summer should be any more sexy than any other time of year. Except... people are walking around with very few clothes on. And of course everyone heads to the beach, where they're wearing even fewer clothes... and everyone's having fun in the park and flirting and drinking and having parties and going to festivals and... oh OK, it is more sexy than other seasons.

With this in mind, perhaps summer is the best time to write that erotic novel you have been promising yourself, to cash in on *Fifty Shades of Grey*. Here is a passage to start you off:

'I need to be tied up,' she breathed. A flush

spread across her face. He looked at her for a moment and then took out a small notebook. 'All right,' he said. 'I'll put you down for meetings all of Thursday and most of Friday morning.'

Actually, writing an erotic novel is a difficult business, because you have to be serious. Humour does not promote arousal; it disperses it. Perhaps the best advice for the aspiring erotic novelist is to bring the whole of life into your erotic novel: the emotions, the intellect, human relations in general. Avoid the merely pornographic. In the famous phrase, the difference between the erotic and the pornographic is that the erotic is using a feather, while the pornographic is using the whole chicken.

98.

FIND CLOUDS THAT LOOK LIKE THINGS

Hamlet played at cloudspotting. 'Do you see yonder cloud that's almost in shape of a camel?' he muses to Polonius. Then he changes his mind. 'Methinks it is like a weasel... or like a whale.' 'Very like a whale,' toadies Polonius.

One can imagine having this conversation for real. 'Do you see yonder cloud that looks like a rhino swallowing a boiled egg?' 'To me it looks like a map of Saskatchewan.' And so on. Clouds are continually changing and morphing into one another. It's a great way to spend a summer's day, flat on your back in a field, staring up at the firmament, chewing on a stalk of grass.

If you're interested in a more scientific approach, the good news is that there are only three basic sorts of clouds: stratus, cumulus and cirrus. Stratus are low clouds that can manifest themselves as fog or mist. Cumulus are the classic cloud shape, flat on the bottom and fluffy on the top. Cirrus clouds form high in the atmosphere from ice crystals, and have a wispy appearance as a result of the much stronger winds up there. Of course, it does get more complicated once one begins to mix the types. Cumulonimbus is everyone's favourite: the towering anvil-shaped cloud associated with storms. Then there are lenticular clouds, a type of lens-shaped cumulus with smooth sides that can be mistaken for UFOs. And the astonishing Fallstreak holes (oval gaps in high cumulus clouds), Mammatus clouds (with lobe-like downgrowths) and iridescent clouds (clouds with rainbow colours that form near the sun). Altogether there are hundreds of sub-types. Grab a cloud atlas and start spotting!

99.

MAKE A TREE-SWING FOR ADULTS

What could be more blissful than to swing high into the sky on a summer's day? Most adults yearn to swing, but are afraid of looking a bit silly. But you must show them the way. Here's how to build a tree-swing that is strong enough to take an adult:

Go to a builder's merchants or hardware store and buy a piece of inch-and-a-half or two-inch thick rot-resistant hardwood such as cedar or maple. Also buy some thick multi-twined plastic rope. The rope should be around an inch thick – the sort of thing you would moor a boat with, not hang washing from.

Cut the wood into a seat ten inches wide and eighteen inches long. Drill holes about an inch and a half from either end, centred. Thread the rope through the holes and tie a thick knot on each rope-end to stop it slipping through.

Find a tree with a branch that is at least ten to twelve inches thick and at least ten feet off the ground (ideally more). Make sure the branch runs roughly parallel to the ground. A higher branch will give a higher ride, so 15-25 feet is better.

Throw the ropes over the branch. If possible, clamber up and drive in guide spikes or eyelets to stop the ropes migrating along the branch when swinging is in progress. Space the ropes a couple of inches further apart on the branch than they are on the seat: this will give added stability. Don't attach the swing too close to the place where the branch forks from the tree, or you will risk hitting the trunk when you swing.

Now put on your best floaty dress (the advice applies to both sexes) and enjoy the summer breeze.

100.

MAKE DAMSON JAM

In late summer in the northern hemisphere, as the days begin to cool, and you begin to wonder 'whether we've had a summer at all this year', what more comforting activity than to make damson jam?

The damson tree blossoms in April and the fruits are ready for picking in late August. The damson is a species of plum, with an astringent taste not generally suitable for eating right off the tree, but perfect for jam-making.

If you want to try it, gather 4 lbs (1.8 kg) of damsons. This will yield 6 lbs (2.7 kg) of finished jam. Wash the fruit and remove any stalks. Then simmer them in a pan with just ¼ pint (145 ml) of water. When the fruit is soft, allow it to cool and then sieve out the stones in a colander. Now add 4 lbs (1.8 kg) of sugar. Stir till this has dissolved, and bring back to the heat. After ten minutes, test the jam to see whether it will set. You can do this by removing a spoonful and laying it on a cool plate: if the jam develops a jelly-like consistency on cooling, you have reached the right balance of water and pulp. Damsons contain a lot of pectin so there's no need to add any. If the jam doesn't set, continue boiling and test again.

Pot it up while the jam is hot (it's more difficult to pot if it has set in the saucepan!). Recycled jam jars are fine as long as they have been thoroughly cleaned and sterilized.

Any damsons left over can be made into damson vodka.

101.

MAKE A SOLAR-POWERED BALLOON

You can only do this in summer, and it's a lot of fun. Essentially, you need four biodegradable bin-bags, some lightweight tape (such as masking tape), and some scissors.

Cut the seam off the bottom of the first bag, getting as close to the seam as you can. Then slit up the side of the bag and open it out. You should now have a rectangle about five feet long and three feet wide. Repeat this with the other three bags and lay them out on the floor in a large square, overlapped by an inch or two where the sides of the bags meet. Then tape them all the way down each side. Now fold the resulting sheet in half, and tape along the two shortest edges of the new shape. Here comes the most difficult manoeuvre. Pinching the midpoint of the remaining open aperture, pull each side outwards to create a tetrahedron (a shape that has four triangular sides and a hollow centre). Tape along the new side. Then pick a corner and cut a small hole. This now forms the bottom of the solar balloon. Turn the whole thing inside out so the seams are on the inside. Inflate the balloon with a hair dryer and you are ready to go. The sun will keep the hot air warm and physics will do the rest.

You can even attach a small camera to the underside of a large balloon (use more bin-bags to make the same shape) and send it up with a tether. Or you can tape an email address to the balloon and see how far it gets.

Avoid trees and airports!

102.

LOOK AHEAD TO AUTUMN

Season of harvests, of plenitude, when all the promise of summer is gathered in. A season for ease and comfort, but also meditation and stock-taking. The poet John Keats imagined Autumn as a person, an androgynous flower-child, too drunk with pleasure even to lift a scythe:

> Who hath not seen thee oft amid thy store?
> Sometimes whoever seeks abroad may find
> Thee sitting careless on a granary floor,
> Thy hair soft-lifted by the winnowing wind;
> Or on a half-reap'd furrow sound asleep,
> Drows'd with the fume of poppies, while thy hook
> Spares the next swath and all its twined flowers:
> And sometimes like a gleaner thou dost keep
> Steady thy laden head across a brook;
> Or by a cyder-press, with patient look,
> Thou watchest the last oozings hours by hours.

Uniquely lost in a sensual bliss, Autumn douses its acolytes not only with opium from poppies but also the hallucinogenic exudations of the apple. In comparison, where are the songs of Spring?

The New Year conventionally begins in January, but it doesn't always feel there's much happening that's 'New'. In reality, the New Year begins in September. Things happen in September: new careers are undertaken, new friendships are forged, new ideas germinate.

Summer is over, but the greatest beauty lies ahead.

THE LITTLE GREY MAN

Identical twins Jerry and Harold Mills are polar opposites. Jerry, hardworking and reliable, has made a success of his life and is engaged to the beautiful Andrea. But his brother soon exhibits his criminal nature and is forced to flee the country and disappear. Five years later, now a murderer and fugitive hiding in Marseilles, Harold writes to his brother, begging him for help. But when the brothers meet, Harold murders Jerry and assumes his identity, faking his own suicide. Then he returns to England, and Andrea . . .